The Real Ma

London Marathon
Everpresents

To Peter another ultra marathoner!

Dale R. Lyons

Best wishes Dale

Bright Pen

Visit us online at www.authorsonline.co.uk

A Bright Pen Book

Copyright © Dale R. Lyons 2014

Cover design by Dale R. Lyons ©

All rights reserved. No part of this publication may be reproduced, stored in a retrieval system, or transmitted in any form or by any means, electronic, mechanical, photocopy, recording or otherwise, without prior written permission of the copyright owner. Nor can it be circulated in any form of binding or cover other than that in which it is published and without similar condition including this condition being imposed on a subsequent purchaser.

British Library Cataloguing Publication Data.
A catalogue record for this book is available from the British Library

ISBN 978-0-7552-1617-8

Authors OnLine Ltd
19 The Cinques
Gamlingay, Sandy
Bedfordshire SG19 3NU
England

This book is also available in e-book format, details of which are available at www.authorsonline.co.uk

TABLE OF CONTENTS
AUTHOR'S BIOGRAPHY...5
SYNOPSIS...6
LONDON MARATHON EVER-PRESENTS..............9
INTRODUCTION...9
CHAPTER 1..12
Making an Ever-present Marathoner.........................12
CHAPTER 2..19
Creating the myth-The early years............................19
CHAPTER 3..30
Disparate Group or a Common Breed?.....................30
CHAPTER 4..67
Gone but not forgotten..67
EVER-PRESENTS MEDIA PRINTS....................108
CHAPTER 5..126
International Globetrotters......................................126
CHAPTER 6..147
Riveting Records around the World........................147
CHAPTER 7..161
Media links to the Marathon Men............................161
CHAPTER 8..172
Ever-presents Charity Contributions.......................172
CHAPTER 9..182
Local Heroes..182
CHAPTER 10..208
A Future for Ever-presents or a Diminishing Breed?
....208
AUTHORS NOTE...222
 A limited audience or a wider appeal?....................222

ACKNOWLEDGEMENTS..223
Appendix 1. Thumbnail memories 1981 – 1995.......224
Appendix 2. Research Survey Form.........................225
Appendix 3 1995 Letter 41 Everpresents 227
Appendix 4 1995 Letter LM Medal..........................228
Appendix 5. 2001 Letter LM plaque........................229
Appendix 6. Letter 2004 Celebration Dinner............230
Appendix 7. Letter BBC TV 'Heroes'......................231
Appendix 8. LM Report 2003 Brasher dies..............232
Appendix 9 London sponsors 1981 2013..................233
Fig. 1 Everpresents 1981 Statistics..........................234
INDEX...235
....243

ISBN 00994 8435 8
Copywrite C Dale R Lyons 2013

AUTHOR'S BIOGRAPHY

Dale was born in North Shields in the North East of England, and then trained as a chef at London's Connaught Hotel. National Service in the RAF and three years in the USA as a chef and restaurant manager followed before he returned to London, and into hospitality management and university lecturing with the Open University. Finally he moved into college management in Birmingham where he lives a contented life with his partner Janet. A London Marathon Ever-present, his leisure pursuits are running marathons playing orchestral banjo as well as clarinet in a blues group.

SYNOPSIS

This is the story of 42 marathon runners who were created as the Ever-presents by the London Marathon in 1995 after they had run 15 consecutive years of the London from the start in 1981.

Their story is a testimony to a *'never say die'* spirit that sustained them during the thousands of marathons they have run all over the world.

Dale Lyons, one of remaining 15, has combined a detailed factual record from his research with the runners with many heart warming anecdotes and astonishing hardship stories to track the Ever-presents journey over 33 years.

Their triumphs and cruel disappointments, the amazing sums raised for countless charities, their startling records at home and abroad and their absorbing and colourful lives away from the marathon treadmill makes for absorbing and enlightening reading.

This is a book to honour their commitment to London, one of the great city Marathons and to provide a lasting tribute to a rapidly diminishing group, decimated by injury, accident, illness and death.

The book will provide information, inspiration, and motivation not only to marathon runners but to those watching the London each year.

FORWARD BY JOHN BRYANT
Author of 'The London Marathon' book and Chairman of the London Marathon Charitable Trust.

This book has been written by one of the Ever-presents – Dale Lyons, known to the running cognoscenti as "The Galloping Gourmet." In it he recalls the battles and struggles these few have had over the years.

To keep going, year after year. these Ever-present runners will try everything and anything. They know all the tricks to keep them going. Jeffrey Gordon found hypnosis could get him to the finish after illness and injury had laid him low. One Ever-present, Dave Martin, ran with a broken toe, a crippled back and wrecked knee. Somehow this elite band managed to battle on through fair-weather and foul, in sickness and in health.

This is certainly the most unique marathon running group in the world. They are an ever dwindling group of London Marathoners who have taken part in every London marathon since its inception in 1981. This group was first acknowledged after the 15th London Marathon in 1995 - when it numbered 42. They were then awarded with a special commemorative medal, a 'T'-shirt and guaranteed entry to future Londons.

The original 42 have now been whittled down, by injuries, illness and death, to 15. They are all male since the first London Marathon had only around 300 women. Obsessive, persistent, lucky, bloody-minded, their prayer is *"Let me do it one more time"*. The youngest at the time back in 1981 was Chris Finill, then aged 22, who went on to be an international athlete of amazing accomplishments, and the oldest Reg Burbidge, then aged 55, finally had to call it a day in 2007 when he was well into his 80s.

Inevitably, this group is now in a race against time itself. It can only be a matter of the passing seasons before they are to be overtaken by *"time's winged chariot"*. There has been much speculation as to who will be the last remaining Ever-present. But of course, with any marathon runner you're only a step away from illness, injury or an accident that might condemn your dreams to oblivion.

Rather like the last Tommy to fight in World War I, there will be much publicity as this band of brothers grows ever smaller. But the truth is that this elite group are now all heroes – marked out by their obsessive courage, stamina and persistence. This remarkable book is a tribute to every one of the Ever-presents. **The London Marathon salutes them all!**

LONDON MARATHON EVER-PRESENTS

INTRODUCTION

Anyone who has run the New York marathon will have the start-line on Staten Island and the towering pillars of the iconic Versarrano Narrows Bridge seared into their memory for all time.

It was in such a place that the seed for The Real Marathon Men book was sown, just before the start of the 1981 New York Marathon and my sixth.

I noticed in front of me a gigantic 10 foot pole held aloft by a rather slight, older runner. The pole was, on closer examination, decorated by a series of running numbers. *"What's that all about?"* I enquired of an American runner. *"Oh that's the famous athlete who has run every New York marathon."* This happened to be the 11th New York marathon and I thought, that is some achievement.

The memory of that day and the iconic picture of the NYC Marathon start line stuck with me ever since.

Then, just year ago I remembered that New York scene again when the **Ever-presents (EPs)** were having the annual group photo at the Green Start and thought, there should be some lasting account of our diminishing numbers; sixteen at that time. But who would take it on, that was the big question? After some thought, the only answer I could think of was - me!

Having just completed my autobiography *'33 Sycamore'* after four years of graft, indecision and intermittent concern that it would never be completed, I knew only too well what an arduous, time consuming project it would be if I decided to bite the bullet and write about the EPs saga.

Well, eventually I did but only after three months heart searching as to whether I really wanted to prioritise my retirement time in this way. More importantly, would I would get the necessary support for the project from the EPs, other individuals and organisations in the mix.

Finally, after a few half hearted attempts making notes and talking to some of the EPs I reached the point of no return. My conscience kept reminding me that *'if I didn't write it no-one else would'* or *'that they (EPs) deserved a lasting tribute'* and *'their story was after all a colourful and unique history of group endeavour'* and *'when it comes down to it, I do enjoy voyages of discovery anyway'*. There were many other reasons but the main ones were well and truly cemented in my mind after reading some of the wonderful and evocative EP's stories. The die was cast!

This book then tells the inside story of a group of runners who were single-minded enough to complete all fifteen London Marathons until 1995 when they were rewarded by Chris Brasher to become the EPs. Now in 2013, with degenerating joints, the ravages of time, injury, illness and death only 15 remain.

Their story makes for a fascinating and compelling insight into the motivation and experiences of the marathon hard-men; **'The London Ever-presents.'** Perhaps the following pages will inspire some of those who watch the London Marathon on TV each year thinking *'that could be me!'*

CHAPTER 1

Making an Ever-present Marathoner

In 1991 EP Rainer Burchett recalls being invited by Chris Brasher to a meeting at the pasta party before the 10th London where a form of Ever-presents (EPs) was discussed but never finalised. 'T' shirts with *'I've run all 10'* were distributed later. At that time there were 90 who qualified including two women. When Rainer asked Chris Brasher if automatic entry would be given to this group, he was given an emphatic *'no!'*, but the seed was sown to blossom five years later.

Eventually a group of 42 runners were given the title *'The Ever-presents'* in 1995 by the London Marathon organisers in recognition of having run every London Marathon. This was during Chris Brasher's tenure as its leading light. They were subsequently given automatic entry each year with the proviso of keeping an unbroken sequence.

Once they had submitted evidence to confirm their fifteen year sequence, they received the gratifying news by letter that they had become a very, very select group. The newly created EPs would still be required to pay the appropriate entry fee but never again would they have to endure the months of nervous anticipation, waiting for a marathon number. The **appendix. 3 Letter** to Mike Peel confirming their EP status, dated 10th August 1995 mentioned only 41 runners that had qualified when by 1996 the number had increased to 42! Where did the extra EP come from and who was it? Did the London Marathon statisticians err or was there some other reason? The answer to this apparent contradiction will be considered later in the book.

It is said that anyone can run a marathon i.e. 26.2 miles, provided they do the training and are willing to suffer, but it takes someone very special who can, over many years overcome not only taxing entry requirements but have the fitness, dedication, stamina and bloody-mindedness to turn up every year, notwithstanding illness and injury to put themselves through a mentally and physically exhausting 26.2 miles. This, mainly for the honour of remaining in what has become a rather exclusive '*club*' of sorts – the **Ever-presents of London**.

These runners are no homogeneous group from a select club. Their common thread, if there is any, is that they are a disparate group, from all parts of the UK and a few from foreign shores, having a wide age range from relative youth to seniors; from a range of social backgrounds and professions and most of them now well past retirement. Some were very good club runners on the elite periphery while others were happy with the occasional PB (personal best time). The EPs marathon times are also as wide as their age range, some well under the 2:30 hour mark and others nearer 4:00 in 1981.

So let us take a good look at these marathon men. What is their story? Why did they start running and then graduate to marathons and ultra distances? Who were their influences and role models? How did they manage to gain a London entry every year – a question many rejected applicants have often asked?

For the first year only 7,741 were entered on a first come first served basis although around four times that number had applied. Of those who ended up in Greenwich Park on the starting line in 1981, some 6,255 finished, about 80% of the starters.

To apply for the first marathon, queues formed at UK's Post Offices all over the country before the midnight deadline before the day entries were to be accepted. Applications were dated, time stamped and progressed by the London Marathon HQ until the allocations were filled. This form of entry favoured those near Post Offices so in later years entries were based on a ballot, the basis of which was not revealed although it was thought that allocations were based on age, gender, predicted running times etc.

Of course there were some anomalies, with some *'early bird'* postal applicants being rejected due to entries being lost or time stamped out of sequence at the point of entry. Appeals from disgruntled applicants however, were sympathetically dealt with in the main by the London management. Elite runners, *'personalities'*, *'fast for age'* candidates and foreign applicants were separately dealt with. Some of the EPs fell into these *'special'* categories while most were just lucky to be accepted for the inaugural event.

Charity Sponsorship by the Ever-presents.

Perhaps EPs motivation to participate was initiated partly by charitable endeavours and if so why did they support the ones they did? Collectively, the EPs have raised six figure sums for various causes over the years and not just through the London Marathon. Many EPs however just wanted to be part of the first premier UK City marathon in London.

London's charity involvement involves hundreds of charities each year who benefit from the thousands who sweat through the 26.2 to raise hard earned cash for these organisations large and small. These charities will also have a view of the EPs direct involvement over the years.

Why then did the London Marathon eventually accord these runners the EP status? Perhaps it was felt by Chris Brasher and his team that an unbroken run of fifteen years was very special and should be formally recognised

Subsequently, over the years there has been some tangible acknowledgement of the EPs status and involvement by the London Marathon hierarchy. A beautifully inscribed medal was presented after fifteen years; see **appendix 4 letter** and a polished wooden, personally inscribed plaque holding two medals after 21 years was sent to each EP; see **appendix 5 letter.** More recently a celebratory dinner was provided for the EPs in London attended by Dave Bedford the London CEO on Saturday 16th April 2004; see **appendix 6 letter.**

London Sponsors

Of course, without a significant input of finances the London Marathon would not have been born or survived beyond 1981 and so a number of international brands supported the marathon with significant sums over the past thirty three years. **Gillette** the US razor giant was the first into the financial breach and currently Richard Branson's **Virgin Money** have take up the baton for the past three years, Richard Branson himself running the first of these in 2010, dressed as a butterfly!

However, these massive sums were not donated purely as philanthropy but to provide a solid base for publicising their products and services, linked to a feel-good mass participation event with significant TV coverage. The question is, did they get their moneys worth from their investment?

Media Involvement.

As with the Marathon sponsors the event would not have survived in its present form without national and international media involvement. Coverage over the years by BBC TV has generated increased participation and interest by the general public, culminating in an annual tourist bonanza that attracts millions to the capital every April.

Completion of the London marathon, as opposed to any other, has a greatly sought after status to the extent that applications greatly outnumber available numbers by a ratio of over 5 to 1 and rising.

The media coverage of the EPs has also been considerable because of their amazing stories and exploits in and out of the marathon. The EPs of London are certainly a phenomenon and their contribution to the London Marathon cannot be overstated.

The gender of the Ever-presents

The gender of the EPs is totally male, so it does not take the investigative powers of a Sherlock Holmes to notice that the original 42 does not contain any women. **See appendix 2. list of 1981 EPs.** Why that is might be tempting to investigate because the London Marathon's Assistant Race Director Nicola Okey says that *"around 300 women were represented in the first London, making up only 5% of the total entry. This would give women only a 20-1 chance of becoming an EP."*

Clearly, no women ran the first 15 Londons consecutively! Low numbers notwithstanding, another reason could be that women in 1981 were mainly between the ages of 30 and 40 and had other competing priorities e.g. raising a family.

Apart from the gender question the book will attempt to provide the fine detail from a number of perspectives of the varied life experiences of the EPs. Additional contributions will be provided by those who have helped to create one of the world's greatest marathons, a truly unique event in the sporting calendar where icons, elites, club runners and wannabees all compete in the same event.

An authors view of the Everpresents

John Bryant, the noted author and writer of the seminal work 'The London Marathon', enthused about the EPs in his book, *"this remarkable group define what is best about the London Marathon, with their prayer of 'Let me do it one more time.'"* This then could be the *cri de coeur* of every EP!

So, in the followed pages, the EPs running endeavours, their records, their media coverage, their charity sponsorship and their non-running family histories, in other words their magnificent experiences, will be laid bare.

CHAPTER 2

Creating the myth-The early years

Among the 7,741 starters of the first London Marathon on the 29th March 1981 were 42 runners who were totally unaware they were to become a group of elites 15 years later, as the London EPs. All the runners were assembled on a foul, rainy day in Greenwich Park to hear Olympic gold medalist and London Marathon creator Chris Brasher CBE, say that they were a privileged group, in that many thousands of runners had been rejected and that he expected this marathon was to become one of the best in the world. What prophetic words!

Thirty three years later the official statistics revealed that over 850,000 had completed the marathon after the 2012 event.

Chris Brasher's inspiration.

Chris Brasher's inspiration had been fuelled by visits to the New York marathon, discussions with its creator Fred Lebow (nee Lebowski) and also to a UK marathon, the first People's Marathon in Birmingham held in 1980 and organised by John Walker the President of the Centurion Joggers Club. The organisation and mass appeal of these marathons made Brasher realise that London as a world renowned city should also have the ownership of a great marathon.

In the first marathon for London some of the future EPs had applied solely because it was the capital's first. They said other marathons simply did not have the same allure or status. As the years have passed it has become more evident that this was the marathon to be involved in. Some of the EPs and their characteristics at that time are worth looking at.

In 1981 the youngest EP was Chris Finill, a youthful 22 year old and the oldest, Reginald Burbidge a mature 55 year old. The remaining 40 were spread across the age range. The fastest EP was Mick McGeoch with an electrifying 2:24:19 while the slowest was Don Martin in 4:10:00, not exactly a pedestrian pace at that. **See fig. 1 EPs 1981 statistics.**

Their stories and the other thirty eight cover amazing marathon journeys around the world, sprinkled with incredible Marathon records, World records, Guinness records, Club records, Race records and not just in marathons.

Research base for the Book.

I had known many of the EPs for almost 30 years, mainly through e-mails and meeting up on London marathon days but it took the completed surveys, (see **appendix 2 research survey)** for me to realise how little of their running lives let alone their personal backgrounds I knew anything about. What a revelation!

The surveys covered the EPs personal, running, sporting, recreational and occupational backgrounds and were the main research tool for the book. Initially they were e-mailed with the surveys and then with follow up phone calls for omissions and additional detail. As the surveys came in further questions were added to provide extra depth and quality to the research e.g. *'What does it mean to be an EP?'* The content of the surveys gave me another massive jolt of enthusiasm for the book. The four EPs not on the internet had their surveys completed by telephone.

The statistical base for the book.

One other factor influenced my decision to write the book. The wealth of detailed statistical information that was available on the Ever-present website was a godsend. Mike Peel, bless him, the web master, had laboured long and hard for many years managing the website with dedication, skill, efficiency and good humour. The background statistics for all the original 42, boosted with personal data and a kaleidoscope of photographs has been zealously updated in a blink, over the years and after each marathon. Substantial statistical support had also been provided initially by Mick McGeoch.

And now, even as Mike moves to a non-active EP status, he has magnanimously agreed to continue as our web master. What a selfless and thoroughly worthy act for which the EPs breathed a collective sigh of relief in the knowledge that the website would continue to provide the central data base for the Eps.

The slippage of marathon times.

In 1981, twenty three of the 42 ran sub 3 hour marathons and only six ran outside 3:30, testifying to the in-depth quality of the group. Thirty three years later times have inevitably slipped away, some more dramatically than others. For Dale Lyons a 3:10 in 1981 crashed to 6:24 in 2013 albeit crutch aided, while Dr Mac Speake's electrifying 2:47 (ranked 12) in 1981 slipped to 7.10 in 2013, ranked last of the survivors but still well inside the 8 hour cut-off time.

Some EPs, much fitter and less prone to the ravages of time and injury have maintained a surprisingly close link to their 1981 times. Chris Finill's blistering time of 2:32:55 in 1981 is surprisingly close to his 2013 time of 2:58:35. That is less than a minute each year! This is all the more amazing as Chris has run **every** London in under 3 hours.

Some others have also kept pace with their 1981 times despite their advancing years. For example, Steve Wehrle has only slipped fifty minutes in thirty three years (3:51 to 4:41). But the most amazing split of all is that of Mike Peace, shedding only twenty three minutes in 33 years (3:11 to 3:34). And at the ripe old age of 64 too!

Training tips
How do they do it - that's the question? Well, staying clear of injury is a good start. Another indicator is keeping race fit and not just by running marathons. Short races of 5 – 10 km developed speed and two to three hour training runs below race pace built stamina, while hill work repeats maintained and improved strength. These were all essential conditions in helping to maintain marathon consistency over the years. A bit of luck in keeping serious illness and injury at bay was also a helpful ingredient. Of course the right diet was crucial for retaining balance within the body's metabolism as well.

Maintaining these factors in the mix could, however be elusive for many runners. Dave Fereday's philosophy, analysed below is worth close inspection in that his marathon training and evaluation system seems to work, for him at least.

An Ever-present's training philosophy
Dave Fereday's log 2013.
'I found that in order to successfully run a marathon in a minimum of time and pain, pace planning is the absolute key. So what pace? Initially before a first marathon one can be guided by how fast, say a fairly hard 20 was run and use this as a yardstick. But then, as training and marathon races progress the required even paced minutes per mile can be better evaluated.

Over the years of the London marathon I have correlated training intensity to marathon times which enables me before each marathon to accurately predict the time. I have recorded from the past 24 Londons each and every mile split and prior to that each ¼ distance split

After each race this data is evaluated to assess how good the pre-race pace planning has been and the reasons if things went wrong. The aim is even paced running throughout, though now at 65 years plus I have had to modify this. I could not physically manage the necessary volume of training that didn't require some running slowdown. However, in my forced conversion to race walking 'even pace' is now again practical.'

N.B. It should be clear from Dave's description that a significant time commitment is required to set up, analyse and maintain this system.

Dave's marathon methodology is set out within his biography in **Chapter 3**.

Benefits of running clubs.

One other feature of the 1981 EPs worth noting was that they were all members of running clubs. A regular request from first time marathoners is *"what tips can you give me for the marathon?"* Join a running club is the best advice by far. A club provides so many essential ingredients for improved running and well-being. Apart from providing a social environment, the other benefits from club membership are legion.

Training advice and free coaching; equipment advice (clothing and shoes particularly); running buddies (usually grouped in speed categories); guided training nights (London Marathon training is mostly in the worst months i.e. November through March) in grade groups gets you out even in the worst weather. Club and presentation nights (for improved status, motivation and recognition); local and national race schedules; reasonable membership fees and discounts for seniors; club discounts at sports shops; access to London Marathon entry numbers (every affiliated club receives an allocation based on club numbers and gives much better entry odds than the London lottery!). And unless you live in the Outer Hebrides there is always a running club not too far away.

Clubs of the Everpresents

The EPs running clubs are spread right across England, Wales and Northern Ireland. There are none living in Scotland although some were born there. Wales have two representatives in Mick McGeoch and Jeff Aston from Cardiff's Les Croupiers with Ken Jones, Northern Ireland's sole representative. There is even one from the USA, Roger Low, another from New Zealand Bill O'Connor, one from Australia Rainer Burchett and finally one from Norway, Erik Falk-Therkelsen.

If you draw lines to separate North & South with Birmingham in the North sector then you find the vast majority of EPs are in the South East, with 83%, and of those almost 50% are in the London area. This statistic might not be too surprising in that London after all is the focal point for the Marathon.

There are five clubs with more than one EP. Orion Harriers with 4, Highgate Harriers 3, Ranelagh Harriers 2, Les Croupiers 2 and Blackheath & Bromley Harriers 2. Harrier clubs have almost 25% of the EPs yet these clubs originally featured short distance runs in a fairly relaxed atmosphere with a culture that espoused the philosophy, *'never let running get in the way of drinking'!* Hardly the rallying cry of hardened marathon runners like the EPs.

It is true however, that many clubs with the Harrier tradition and those based on track and field athletics have seen the writing on the economic wall and opened their doors to previously shunned athletes; long distance runners!

Memories of the early Londons.

Three EPs from the harrier tradition recall some memorable experiences from the inaugural 1981 London. Dave Clark almost missed the start along with eight others who found the Kensington tube closed and hot-footed towards Earls Count where they commandeered a six seated taxi. Taking pity on hearing their plight, the driver took all nine with three crouching out of sight on the floor so they could get to the start on Blackheath in time. They eventually made it with thirty minutes to spare. It was the start of many more Londons for Dave!

By contrast Steve Wehrle wasn't even sure he could complete the first London as the furthest he had run was around sixteen miles. He had only started running three years earlier to get fit and although he hit a bad patch around eighteen miles he finished in a very respectable 3:51:26 and never looked back. Additionally he recalls that in 1981 a really lonely part was the 6 mile loop around the Isle of Dogs. Now it is heaving with charity groups, local residents, runners' families and spectators!

Dale Lyons remembers running the first London alongside a Swiss waiter Roger Bourbon carrying a tray on which was a bottle of Perrier and a water-glass. *"He was so fast I couldn't keep up and found out later he was an Olympic runner on the Swiss team!"* He also remember stopping at the Tower of London to give a glucose tablet to the Blue Peter presenter Peter Duncan as he had hit *'the wall'* *. He finished in his fastest time to date, 3:10:03, but still lagged Peter by a minute at Buckingham Palace.

* *'Hitting 'The Wall'* is the physiological state of inertia when the body runs out of glycogen (glucose energy) and seems to hit an invisible wall. The muscles can store about 2,000 calories and a runner uses about 100 calories per mile so without any supplements the 20 mile mark becomes the negative carbohydrate threshold. However, a small amount of rest or sugar in the form of glucose, carbohydrate drinks, or even jelly babies, will provide a short term energy *'hit'* and get you going.

The London was Rainer Burchett's third after the Masters & Maidens marathon, just missing out on a sub

3 hour with a 3:00:51. However, he made a sub 3 hour in his next marathon in 2:58:30, the first London, in 1981. Twenty five years later he came across the Masters results and discovered another EP just ahead of him in 4th place, Pat Dobbs!

Before Alastair Aitken's first London he recalls being very nervous after seeing the massive TV publicity the day before because his previous marathon in Cambridge was watched *"by about 100 spectators"*. He survived with a sub 3 hour London due to the support of his friend Ron Wheeler, his wife Joanna, son Andrew and then celebrated with a bottle of Krug Champers at the finish! Cheers Alastair!

In 1981 Dave Fereday kept a log detailing expected against actual time with a percentage success rating for each and a brief summary of what went right or wrong.. This log has been kept for every London since. What dedication!

From 1981 – 1995, in the years before the EPs were born, Dale Lyons kept a thumbnail sketch of each marathon with his time and a notable feature of those years. For example, he remembers 1981 as *"3:10 My P.B. by 30 minutes! Freezing cold & rain. The first marathon dead heat. Dick Beardsley & Inge Simondsen. I ran for a few miles with the 'Perrier' waiter who volunteers to flambé the pancake!"* And the 1995 entry *"3:58:33 New World 3 Legged Record. Dave Pettifer drags me round for a new 1996 Guinness Book entry."* See **appendix 1 1981 – 1995 A Reminisce of Running Idiocy,** for the remaining thumbnails.

All the EPs hailed the first London a big hit and resolved to return in 1982, provided they could get an entry number. Not an easy option at that time. So, of the hundreds of thousands who had run the London in the first fifteen years only 42 remained who had completed them all. **The London Ever-presents were born!**

CHAPTER 3

Disparate Group or a Common Breed?
Fifteen runners hanging in after 33 years

The EPs are nothing if not varied in all sorts of ways so let us look in detail how a group of such variety had at the same time two distinct assets. They were good at running long distances, even better at running 26.2 miles but in most other respects had little in common. See **Fig. 1 EPs 1981** Statistics. Their only commonality seems to centre on the psychological need to run long, painful and physically draining distances.

The following quote by Geoff Wightman- London Marathon finish line announcer and MD of runbritain sums up the character trait of the EPs.

"With every year that passes since 1981, the magnitude of the achievement of the Marathon Ever-Presents grows and grows. How can it be that every April, in sickness and in health, in fair weather and foul, they have made an unbreakable date with the longest run that the Olympic programme has to offer and come out ahead? I trained with Chris Finill for ten years so I am aware that behind the classic distance there are some classic tales that will be enhanced further as the years go on because these are uncommon characters. Congratulations to Dale for recording it all while the story is still unfolding."

Ever-presents mileage and distances

One thing that this research makes clear is that being a club member clearly demonstrates a dedication and a commitment to running and what running there has been. Just trawl through the variety of distances the EPs have covered in their CV's; 5k; 10k; 5 mile; 10 mile; half marathon (13.1 miles); 15 mile; 20 mile; 21 mile; Marathon; Double Marathons (Comrades in South Africa); Double & Triple Londons (unofficial); 100k; 24 hour runs; 52 miles (London – Brighton); Trans Americas i.e. 3,000 miles and a host of cross country ultra marathons. The mind boggles at this spread of distances for such a small group.

Just reading about these runs would make most people weary! It is also true to say that many more miles have been covered in non marathon running. If you add up all the miles run in both marathons and non-marathon races you would still be many thousands of miles short when you count all the training miles completed. For example Dale Lyons calculated that of the 42,000 odd miles he has run, only 5,000 were in races, a ratio of 7 – 1. And, less than 25% of his 401 races were over the marathon distance.

Put simply, training for a marathon in particular requires an input of hundreds of miles. Quite a commitment for club runners and then consider the mileage of full time athletes such as Mo Farah and Paula Radcliffe who are training over 120 miles weekly!

The fifteen EPs running and sporting biographies which follow are listed in the order of their finishing positions in the 2013 London. The asterix identifies those EPs who completed the research survey and the time given in the heading is their fastest recorded marathon..

* CHRIS FINILL   2:28:27
Chris Finill runs for Harrow AC and Thames Hare & Hounds with his second claim club the Road Runners Club of London with whom he has regular links. Chris is one of the fastest EPs and in his first London ran a very quick 2:32:55, but in 1985 he ran his best, in 2:28:27. He put this gift for running down to doing fast laps around his garden when he was a youngster and getting his mother to keep count.

During one of his London Marathons in the 1980's Chris recognised a familiar face in the line-up and caught up with him after 800 yards to have a closer look. Sure enough, the runner he had just recognised was none other than the double Olympic Gold Medalist from the Montreal games, the one and only Alberto Juantorena. It certainly made Chris's day.

His marathon haul of '*55 ish*' does not include a number of ultra runs, and if they were would add significantly to the total. Another ultra runner with whom he ran in the GB ultra squad was a certain Hilary Walker, a world record performer and someone who could have been a female EP as she has completed more than 25 Londons.

Laid up with flu in 1998 he rallied enough to get to the start and just managed to duck under the 3 hours mark in 2:57:56 for his 2nd slowest London. A much more enjoyable one was in 2012 when he ran a * **negative split** in a time of 2:50:32 and his fastest in five years.

His other exploits read like a who's who of runnings crème de la crème. For example, has any marathon runner maintained sub 3 hour marathon times for five decades, 1970 – 2013? Unbelievably, Chris has, along with a very select group worldwide and only three in the UK!

His ultra runs include representing England & Great Britain 14 times in 100k (62 miles) and 24 hour races. His record over the years from 10k to marathons in AAA / Welsh and International championships clearly indicates an elite performer par excellence!

* **A negative split** is when you run the second half of a race faster than the first and is extremely difficult to achieve in a marathon.

Chris really values being a member of the EPs and says it gives him a goal and a structure each year. The attendant media interviews are an enjoyable bonus but, he reflects, tongue firmly in check *"it would have been a lot easier if I'd have missed one of the early Londons, although the pressure (of being an EPs) does give context and purpose to the training three decades down the line"*. He is also a world traveller having raced on five continents.

One of his crowning achievements was to lead home a trial group of 35 runners who were testing the 2012 Olympic marathon route finishing in the Mall. He is definitely our EP *'maillot jaune'* and still only 54.

MIKE PEACE   2:40:14

Mike Peace of Ranelagh Harriers ran his first London in 3:11:45 and is one of the EP *'youngsters'* at 63. Chris Brasher and London Marathon winner Hugh Jones were his club mates – exalted company indeed!.

Of the first 22 Londons Mike ran 20 in sub 3 hour times, the fastest at 2:40:14 in 1994. Mike's consistent times over the past 10 Londons have been remarkable, rarely varying more than half a minute around the 3:30 mark. He finished his 33rd in 3:34:01 and was second only to Chris Finill. So far he has run 45 marathons around the world and these include two ultras in South Africa.

As with his marathon times his short distances are just as impressive with a half marathon in 1:13; 10 mile in 53 minutes; 10 km in 33 minutes and 5 miles in 27:50. Mike counts one of his more memorable training sessions in Richmond Park, accompanying a fifteen year old Mo Farah!

His worst marathon experience was walking for about 2 miles in the Heart of England Marathon with stomach cramps but still finished in 2:39 for 10th place! Mike's Ranelagh team had three runners in the top ten but needed four to win the team prize; how frustrating!

Some of his most enjoyable annual shorter distance races with a competitive edge were the *'mob matches'*. These matches, held annually involve a group of the oldest running clubs in the country, comprising Mike's club Ranelagh Harriers 1881, Thames Hare & Hounds 1867, South London Harriers, and Blackheath & Bromley Harriers.

Although some of his friends and family consider him *'completely nuts'* he thinks that being an EP is a privilege and not a burden. *"It's a unique band of runners in a club you can only leave. We can do our part in making a continuing connection to the unique quality of the (London) race"*

* ROGER LOW   2:33:47

Another fast EP is Roger Low of Highgate Harriers who ran the first London in 2:47:55 then had an electrifying 2:33:47 as his fastest. marathon in London 1983.   At 69 Roger is in the mid age range of the remaining 15 EPs. and considers his best marathon as *'any-one that I've finished'*.   He has now run *'about'* 100 marathons worldwide and considers London spectators are on a par with New York.   They used to be his favourite.

An impressive statistic for Roger's Londons was finishing the first fourteen in sub 3 times. He is pretty quick over ultra distances too in finishing the London-Brighton run in a very impressive 6:45.

* JEFF ASTON   2:29:34

One year after becoming an EP Jeff Aston became a founder member of Les Croupiers of Cardiff (sounds French) along with Mike McGeoch. Then in the 1983 London Jeff ran his fastest in a blistering 2:29:34, one of the fastest EP times and not far behind the women's winner, the famous Grete Waitz! In that race he was 285th overall but Jeff calculates that with the gradual erosion of marathon times he would probably be inside the first fifty today.

He recalls a memorable award he received after his first and second Peoples Marathon in Birmingham and the first mass participation marathon in 1980, a year before London. His inaugural time was a very respectable 4:21 but his second, was a quick sub 3 in 2:53. Jeff was rewarded with a magnificent silver tray compliments of Unisys Computer Systems, one of the sponsors. It still holds pride of place among his many trophies. In fact, in his first year he ran two other marathons, the Newport in 3:35 and the tough Masters & Maidens in 3:21.

In the first London he received another prize of a little more use, stemming from an advert in the Marathon Magazine for Deep Heat the muscle rub. The advert offered the advice on *'how to finish 765th'*. Jeff duly finished 765th and on informing Deep Heat's Customer Services he received a years supply of their product!

As Jeff is a seriously quick marathoner his shorter races are also impressive with a half marathon in 1:10:56 in Barry in 1983 at the tender age of 35 and an equally fast 10 miles of 52:51 in the same year. Short distances are also quick with 10k in 33:08; 5 miles in 26:46; 5k in 16:18 and the mile in 4:57, all ran in his home town of Cardiff in the mid 1980's.

His fast times came to an abrupt end in millennium year due to severe back spasms. Not intending to relinquish his EP status without a fight, Jeff walked the 26.2 miles in a pedestrian 5:38:30 and finished last EP. Jeff admits rather shamefacedly that it was his own fault as he had run two twenty mile road races six days apart only three weeks earlier! Silly boy!

Jeff's real claim to fame is that he is the only runner in Wales to have run every London, according to a Radio Wales interview in 2009. Would Mick McGeoch, another Welshman, have something to say about that if he hadn't dropped out after 2002?

Maybe lack of training preceded his worst marathon experience when he *'hit the wall'* in the 1982 London and still finished in 2:48:13! One is left to wonder what time he would have done if he hadn't. His advice to wannabe marathoners is *"don't short-change on training because you'll suffer for a long time"* Jeff has now completed 55 marathons and as one of the surviving EPs, intends to keep up the London sequence for some time yet.

His other sports included skiing, squash and football before he started his real love of running. Jeff started in 1980 because his local squash court was flooded and he had to find another way to keep fit.

Jeff sometimes cannot believe he is an EP until he reads about himself in the papers which tends to make him a star among the local runners. He is very proud he says of *"being in a Club no-one else can join"*. A club even Groucho Marx couldn't belong!

Outside of running 70 miles in training, Jeff, now a youthful 66 still has time for organising the Gwent Cross Country League's website statistics. Being a retired IT Systems Analyst he has also helped to head up one of the largest leagues in the world! To cap it all Jeff still runs cross country races and has an unbroken sequence of 158 (5 per season) over 31 years – what a record!

STEVE WEHRLE   2:59:59

One of the younger EPs at 65, Steve Wehrle of Dulwich Runners AC is still hanging on with a very respectable 4:41:29 in 2013. Another sub 3 hour EP by just one second was his fastest in the 1991 London with a 2:59.59. This contrasts with his worst experience in 2010 when a severe bout of sciatica forced him to walk most of the 26.2 in a relaxed time of

41

6:39:04. Just shows the agony he suffered to retain his EP status!

He vividly remembers his first London, run in a commendable time of 3:51:26 where the Isle of Dogs was almost empty. So far he has completed 45 marathons in the UK and on foreign soil and intends to keep going.

Steve is also a bit of a walker, having laboured on the Coast to Coast (St.Bees to Robin Hood's Bay), a small matter of 196 miles in fourteen days. Maybe his other BBC interests kept his mind off the pain? In 2001 before the 20th London, Steve, BBC's own running guru was interviewed on BBC TV Sports-line and gave the following *'top tip'* on marathon running.

"Do not scrimp on training – do the mileage! Train with friends and mix your sessions up. Take it steady at the start; save some gas for Docklands" Having already run the trifling total of 45,000 miles in training and races, he is well placed to provide good advice. Steve is also handily placed for his next London, living as he does in Orpington, Kent.

* CHARLES COUSENS   2:55:29

Charles Cousens, of the Vale of Aylesbury club, had a rather quickish time of 2:55:29 for his fastest London and at 70 years is still running the Marathon in under 5 hours.

He has completed 49 marathons around the world, among which was the *'very tough'* Seven Sisters near Beachy Head and the Masters & Maidens over Surrey's Hogs Back in 3:43.   He recalls chatting to Steve Redgrave our five times Olympic gold medallist after the Masters and told him about his EP status to which Steve replied *'you must be bloody mad!'*

Charles' CV also includes some of the top international marathons but he is quick over the shorter distances as well, with a half marathon in 1:19:27. In the early years of the London he recalls enjoying meeting up with his club mates, sitting on the grass in Green Park and *"having fun and a good laugh"*

He cannot recall a *'worst marathon experience'* and says he enjoys them all which must make him an exception. Charles also competes in short distance triathlons, ten to date, and recently completed one at Fountains Abbey at the mature age of seventy one.

One of the UK's toughest off road multi-terrain races is the Tough Guy '8' near Wolverhampton and in the early 1990's he completed five of them. Usually, one would put most runners off permanently!

* BILL O'CONNOR   2:34:29

One of our fastest EPs Bill O'Connor of Queens Park Harriers, ran the first London in the fifth fastest time of the original 42 with a 2:35:52 rocket and is immensely proud to be one of the surviving EPs.

He recalls having to register for the 1981 marathon at Swan & Edgar near Piccadilly Circus and then having to wait five minutes to cross the start line in Greenwich Park. This was well before computer chips triggered runners' time as they crossed the start line.

During the inaugural race he recalls the amazing atmosphere among the runners, most of who had never participated in a mass marathon; Alastair Aitken made the same point. There were few if any spectators on many parts of the City and East End especially around the Isle of Dogs and Docklands.

The marathon route has had alterations in most years occasioned by the mega developments on the Isle of Dogs, Canary Wharf, DLR (Docklands Light Railway) and around the Tower of London where by avoiding the strip of cobbles the course has been made marginally faster.

Bill's fastest time was in the 1985 London in an elite time of 2:34:29 which he said was "*my most enjoyable, with great weather and so well organised by the London Marathon team*" Bill was a real *'Boy Scout'* before the first London, stopping to pick up London runners at bus stops on his way from North London. *"I could spot they were runners by the bags they were holding"* enthuses Bill. It must have been his Kiwi community upbringing in lending a helping hand.

Some of his slower marathon times were not through any lack of training but because of a road accident. In October 1989 Bill was knocked off his bike by a BMW that swerved into a parking slot, giving him a recurring neck injury and worst of all a 3:13:55 time in the marathon. Any other runner would consider that time acceptable, but not in Bill's book.

Then in 2001 he damaged his cruciate ligament after falling in the Watford half Marathon and '*crawled*' around that year's London in his slowest time of 5:31:55. Overall, Bill has now completed 38 marathons all in the UK, his adopted home. His first two marathons were in the iconic Polytechnic runs where he cut his teeth. He has also run the Isle of Wight marathon twice and the Kodak, all of these well under the 3 hour mark.

Marathons apart, Bill's shorter distances would have most runners drooling. With 20 miles in 1:53:12; a ½ marathon in 1:10; a 10 miles in 51:29; a 5 mile in 24:40; 880 in 1:58; 440 in 52.7 and best of all a mile in 4:16. These really are elite performances.

His other sporting pursuit was playing rugby in New Zealand and this lead to a serious face injury when he was seventeen so he took up the less physical sport of football. Good call Bill! It was here that he started running to lose some pounds. Weighing in at 14 stone he entered a number of ten mile races then graduated to 20 mile training runs which eventually trimmed him down to 8½ stone – job done – but the running bug had taken hold.

During his time in New Zealand's South Island Bill used to train in bare feet running along the Tasman Sea beaches in near Blaketown where he taught for five years and had views of Mount Cook, their tallest mountain.

Initially, marathon distances did not appeal to Bill, preferring the shorter distances for his weekly 100 training miles. After taking some stick from running colleagues he graduated to 20 mile runs, achieving some very quick times of under two hours, his first of 1:58:30 in the Finchley 20. He regrets staying off the marathon distances when he was in his 20's and thinks a 2:30 marathon time would have been possible. Bill has made up for it since!

Being an EP means a great deal and he considers it is a great honour to have been able to run all 33 so far. And because of this he was always determined to finish and never, ever got bored.

Another great honour to be bestowed on Bill was on the 25th July 2012. He had the enormous privilege of carrying the Olympic Torch through the streets of Haringey, adjacent to Alexandra Palace, the early home of the BBC, on day 68 of the Relay.

* DAVE FEREDAY 2:44:12

Dave Fereday of Barnet & District AC & Redcar Race Walking Club and a Geordie by location ran eight of the first eleven Londons in under 3 hours. His first London in 3:12:52 was his first *'proper'* marathon, which he ran with a dodgy back after osteopathy treatment only 2 weeks before; mind over matter perhaps? Dave's motivation was in the genes, it seems, he was *'born to run'* as he tells his story.

"I had been born a runner. Since I toddled I seemed to (want to) run. Run to the shops, through the woods, round and round the school playground– never walked anywhere. I won the schools cross country championship against much older boys but nobody said I should join the local harriers – such was the hit and miss approach of weaning (running) ability."

The year Dave became an EP he hit the wall at 18 miles and only managed 3:40:33, almost 20 minutes outside his forecast, due he said to the stifling heat and *"one of the hottest marathons"* and concludes this was *"marathon pain at its very worst"*. Even so, a sub 4 hour marathon is no disgrace even to a runner of Dave's pedigree.

He is one of our most dedicated marathon recorders, detailing each London with meticulous care (see an extract from his log below for 1996, the year after EP recognition.)

<u>1996 – Age 58</u>
Target time/pace 3.21.00 - 7.40/mile – Fit to that of 1994 makes this target look easy

Actual 3.40.33 – 8.26/mile - each quarter 7.28 7.39 8.21 10.18
When the 'wall' came Mile 18 - 8.21 then painful deterioration to 10/11 minutes/mile
Prior training history 32 week average 25, 8 week average 34, Fitness factor 29.5
Comments
Can only conclude bad performance due to heat. This was the hottest 'London' ever after a long spell of cold weather. This was marathon pain at its very worst. Why O why do we do it?

In 1985 he ran his fastest London, in a seriously quick time of 2:44:12, age 47.

So far he is over half way to completing 100 marathons with 55 at home and abroad but doubts if he will get to a century. His shorter distance times are equally impressive with a half marathon in 77:30; 10 miles in 56:47 and a 10k in 34:30 while he was in his mid forties.

Dave is a very handy speed walker too and has completed the gruelling 85 Mile Isle of Man Parish Walk twice, as a member of Redcar Race Walkers. In 2011 as a youthful 72 year-old he completed the course in 21:21 and beat the 70+ record by 31 minutes. He took up this new sport after the 2008 London when his knee cartilage wore out and decided to preserve his EP status by race walking.

Dave is also a dab hand at tennis, winning the RAF doubles during his RAF National Service in the 1960's and competing in a match with the British #3 at the time. He still plays table tennis competitively in the Northumbria league and takes a keen interest in golf, if only on a 19 handicap.

Being an EP Dave says *"is the main target of my life and the all pervading reason for training and carrying on!"* A pretty strong affirmation and no tongue in cheek.

* TERRY MACY   2:58:18

Terry Macy ran for New Eltham Joggers for 15 years with his fastest marathon in the London in 2:58:18, and another sub 3 EP. He has racked up a total of forty marathons, many of them in very attractive cities all over the world.

In 2009 he was encouraged to accompany his daughter on her first marathon in a time of 4:30 and counts this as his favourite, having trained hard and felt comfortable all the way. His worst by far was the London's of 2012 and 2013 when a ruptured tendon required a knee operation and then cruciate ligament damage slowed him down to times of 5:38:53 and 5:45:02 respectively. On this evidence EPs don't give up easily!

One enjoyable marathon took in the three counties of Essex, Sussex and Suffolk so not surprisingly it was called – you've guessed it – The 3 Counties Marathon. He cannot remember his time so he must have enjoyed it. His shorter distances are also worth a mention with 1:03 for 10 miles and 1:18 for the ½ marathon.

Terry recalls a memorable training run in Southwark Park and an interesting encounter just before the 1981 Marathon. Turning into the park he almost ran into Chris Brasher, unaware that Chris was being filmed for the first marathon documentary. The BBC camera crew were rather miffed at having to redo the action, as was Christopher!

Terry lives only 400 yards from the Marathon Green start on Shooters Hill SE7 so he can probably have a lie-in on race days unlike most other runners- what a bonus!

His major non running recreation riding his British made Raleigh bicycle. He rode with a group to Switzerland three times in 2004, 2009 and 2013. That sounds like a very long bike ride and hard work. Terry is obviously as enthusiastic on a bike as he is in trainers!

What it means to be an EP according to Terry is, *"to keep running all year and once a year to meet friends and family to share the enjoyment of the weekend of the marathon. I think people share my belief that I have been very fortunate to have had the health to be marathon fit for 33 years".*

* DAVID WALKER   2:45:30

David Walker of Chiltern Harriers had a 2:45:30 as his fastest marathon in the 1987 London. He has now completed about 39 *"but could be more"*.

His most enjoyable run was the 2005 London where he ran with his three children, which accounts for his relatively slow time of 6:20:05, but was this just an excuse?

His first London was memorable in that he finished in 3:06:11, ahead of the Blue Peter presenter Peter Duncan, a TV celebrity at the time.

We all have marathons to forget and David's worst was in 2012 when a back strain virtually immobilised him. *"I was struggling from five miles and in the end was relieved to finish in what was for me a pedestrian time of 6:30:24."* He remembers this with grim satisfaction as he managed to retain his EP status. This he feels is an integral and important part of his family life although it tends to get in the way of other activities. Many of the EPs have made the same observation. *"Why do I put myself through this 26.2 miles torture every year? I can't really think of a good reason!"*

David must have worried about this very point in one marathon when his '*bleed out*' diet went somewhat awry. He consumed 6 double size Mars bars to carbo load little realising that chocolate is quite a good laxative. At the 23 mile mark he suddenly found out and had to do a quick AWOL similar to Paula Radcliffe 's London at about the same stage. No-one volunteered to shake his hand at the finish!

In the 2009 London he was running with his 32 year old son Andrew who finished in 3:35 but ran a little too fast and ended up in the St. John's recovery tent. When David went to check on his recovery all his son could say was *"Dad, why didn't you take up fishing?"* Good point!

* DALE LYONS 2:57:15

Dale Lyons aka 'The Galloping Gourmet', an ex pat Geordie who has gone almost full circle with his running clubs, starting with Centurion Joggers, Massey Ferguson AC, and Sphinx AC (Coventry). His first London in 3:10:03 was his third marathon after the 1st Peoples in Birmingham and the Masters & Maidens in Surrey.

Dale started jogging to get fit to play squash because he realised *"you don't get fit playing squash but you've got to be fit to play"*, but after getting bored jogging through the streets of Solihull he joined the Centurion Joggers and recalls his first run. *"I was introduced to a group of five older men and women and thought 'they don't look like runners'. They started off chatting and doing 6 mph – I couldn't keep up!"*. Although his quickest marathon was 2:57:15 in the Wolverhampton Marathon his fastest London was 3:06:42 tossing pancakes!

His running total of 92 marathons does include some ultras but he is not optimistic of reaching the century. Some of his more eccentric Londons had Dale dressed as a Bustard (an extinct big bird now being reintroduced in Britain) and then carrying a zimmer frame all the way for Age Concern in 2006.

One of his worst marathon experience was attempting a triple London Marathon in 1997. After the first two in 4:37 and 5:28 he reached the Isle of Dogs at about 9 pm during the third and ran out of steam. The next year in 1998, he finally completed the first triple London in a total time of 17:12 for the 78.6 miles. Dale has also run three double Londons as well as the triple so does this mean he has run five more than any EP, i.e. 38?

Dale's most enjoyable was his first New York Marathon in 1981 where it seemed the whole of New York was afflicted with marathon fever. A five mile breakfast run from the United Nations the day before had every nation's flag leading their respective runners up 5th Avenue and into Central Park where a magnificent breakfast buffet had been set up. What a feast!

His shorter run times are 5 miles in 28:43; 10 miles in 59:59!; 10k in 36:30 and a ½ marathon in 1:17 so he is no pedestrian.

Dale's other sporting interests included triathlons, skiing, snowboarding, squash and football. He also competed for five years in the Karrimor Mountain Marathon, a two day paired orienteering event, usually held in inhospitable areas of the Lake District and Scotland, a race that really separates the wheat from the chaff.

He was also selected for the British team (age related) in the World Triathlon Championships in Manchester in 1990 and finished thirteenth in his age group... *"The Manchester weather did not cooperate"*, he said. Then, biting the ultra bullet, he entered the first UK Ironman in 1991 and was pleased with his time of 12:48.

It was while he was on his RAF National Service that he played football for Bomber Command HQ winning the RAF Senior Cup in 1962, albeit with a little help from two of Chelsea's first team.

Being an EP has almost become a crusade for Dale and sometimes he has nightmares about being late for the start. *"I'm immensely proud of being in such illustrious company (as the other EPs)"* says Dale. That is what keeps him turning up each year, with or without a crutch!

* JEFF GORDON 2:42:00

Jeff Gordon is a runner for Thames Hare and Hounds and is known affectionately as *'Flash Gordon'*. John Bryant, the noted author and club Captain, encouraged Jeff to start running. Ungraciously, Jeff then beat him in the 1981 Honington Marathon in 2:42, his fastest time and was just pipped into 3rd place. He also had the better of two illustrious club runners, Chris Chataway and Roger Bannister, back in the 1980's in two cross country events. Memories to cherish!

Jeff is another sub 3 hour runner with a string of seven London to Brighton races to his credit, the best in 7:10. His first London was a sprightly 3:13.42 with his fastest of 2:49:54 in 1982. He has now run over 100 marathons, including ultras which include the Woodford 40 mile in 5 hours and the Lincoln to Grantham 100k in just over 10 hours. No wonder his wife Shirley calls him *'bonkers'*.

Another notable run was in the Worthing 20 when he was given hypnotherapy by his wife Shirley to overcome a recurring leg strain by visualising the calming colour of yellow. This, Jeff said worked a treat as the run was in March and the daffodils were out all along the route.

Taking up cross country running in his early 40's had a beneficial side effect that came in handy for Jeff one day in Balham's youth court. After a felon on trial escaped from court, Jeff, a trial lawyer, gave chase across a busy South London road and eventually apprehended the youth until the court police arrived.

On another occasion, as related in John Bryant's book The London Marathon, Jeff started the marathon alongside a suspended policeman who he had helped to convict in the famous *Christmas Tree Bribery Case*. The Bobby hoped Jeff *'would drop dead'* (in the marathon) but typically Jeff did one of his best times!

As with all EPs, he slowed to 6:53:02 in 2013 but finished strongly and is determined, naturally to stay an active EP, as are the other fourteen! Jeff is immensely proud to be an EP but it can sometimes be rather embarrassing as the judges in chambers take a keen interest in his London marathon exploits and pepper him with questions about his times and progress.

* 'DOC' MAC SPEAKE   2:44:50

One of the two MD's in the EPs group 'Doc' Mac Speake of Biddleston Bounders AC is one of our dedicated ultra runners. He survived the South Downs Way twice in a time of 13:15; a 100k run in 7 hours and the London to Brighton a 53 mile run in a sub 7 hour time.

He can, however, speed up occasionally and has an impressive 2:44:50 for his fastest marathon. A back problem was the reason for his slowest and worst marathon experience in a time of 7:10:20 in 2013.

In 1983 despite a fast 2:49 Mac said he was passed by a Swiss waiter carrying a tray and a bottle of Perrier water with only 100 yards to go, how embarrassing! Mind you this waiter was a member of his country's Olympic team! (see Dale's experience in his biog. with the same waiter, Roger Bourbon)

'Mac' can be counted as a very serious and competent marathon runner on the evidence of his first fifteen Londons, thirteen of which he ran in sub 3 hour times. He also prefers the UK marathons, having completed all of his 120 on British soil. A true Anglophile.

Besides Marathons, Mac also runs fast over shorter distances with the following impressive times. A 10k in 36:00; 10 miles in 60:30 and a ½ marathon in 1:19. He has also volunteered as an Athletics Course 1 Measurer since 1983 with over 100 courses to his credit.

Among Mac's other sporting pursuits are triathlons and tandem cycle touring – very good but who's in front doing the hard work?

Mac's view on being an EP has a medical slant; *"it's a bloody obsession, a compulsive disorder!"* He adds, *"I wouldn't run (London) if I were not an EP but it's a "real status symbol and given the opportunity I do swank about it"* Well, if you've got it, flaunt it Doc!

PAT DOBBS 2:31:38

Pat Dobbs of Thurrock Harriers is one of the quick EPs with his fastest London in 2:31:38. He is now a sprightly 74 and another model of consistency because after 23 Londons was still running sub 3's at 63, the last, in 2003 in an amazing 2:57:36.

KEN JONES   2:55:38

Ken Jones, one of four Orion Harrier EPs with his fastest London in 2:55:38 in 1985. His 1981 time was 3:18:37 and his slowest, by only five minutes in 5:55:52 was in 2013. Ken is our only Northern Irish EP.

He also had the honour in 2012, age 78 of carrying the Olympic Torch. His stage, through the packed streets of Strabane in Northern Ireland was *"a day in a million"* despite a spectator making a failed attempt to grab the torch from him en route. Our Irish hero was having none of it and carried on to the renewed cheers of the packed ranks of spectators. Ken was fulsome in his praise for the Police and Olympic Relay Team and added his thanks to his EP friend, Roger Low for nominating him.

Chapter 3 Summary

Of the fifteen active EPs, thirteen have contributed to the research for the Real Marathon Men with the EPs website information, statistics and external sources used to provide additional detail for their biographies. These include only their UK sporting interests, statistics and club details. Additional information on their records, international runs, media coverage, charity involvement and family lives are covered in subsequent chapters.

It seems clear from the EPs biographies that they are in most respects a disparate group of runners, as the chapter title suggests. Although all now live in Britain some of the EPs have come from some distance away to continue their running sagas in the UK for a variety of reasons.

Some started running through a related sport like rugby; or by family example; by something in the genes; or due to a valued role model; perhaps to get fit for another sport or even to lose weight. Once sampled however, running became their chosen lifelong sporting activity.

Many examples are given which indicate that their journey to the marathon distance started from shorter runs, but rarely did these provide the challenge that their abilities and motivation needed for fulfilment.

Marathons have been and probably always will be, the Holy Grail of long distance running and the first London Marathon was an example of that. The iconic route, the mass participation and media coverage satisfied not only the challenge but the grand stage on which the EPs could and did perform. As some discovered however, there were concerns as to their preparedness to run 26.2 miles at the first asking.

Their running and sports biographies clearly show, in some detail a variety of differences in their makeup. With one exception, all have run sub 3 hours in the London, testifying to their high level of ability and fitness. A few have, knowingly doubled up on the 1996 Centenary Boston and London Marathons in the same week, and survived!

Most have completed a range of ultra marathons, from the Comrades, 100k, London to Brighton, Double and Triple marathons and even to crossing America! Many have represented their country with distinction in marathons, ultras and in shorter distances, with some on the track.

The time gap in 2013 between first and last EP was a little over 4 hours. Time perhaps for Chris (Finill) to run another 26.2? In 2013 only one EP broke 3 hours (Chris Finill), one ran under 4 hours; five under 5 hours; four under 6 hours; three under 7 hours and one under 8 hours. This year sadly, one failed to finish, our webmaster Mike Peel. Au revoir Mike.

CHAPTER 4

Gone but not forgotten

Chapter 4 analyses the non-active EPs with their stories of good fortune and heartbreak. Out of the original 42 in 1981 three EPs have unfortunately died. John Legge of Orion Harriers and Chris Adams also of Orion Harriers both in 2001 and Max Jones of Birchfield Harriers in 2010.

Some are not in the best of health and two have Parkinson's Disease. It is a testimony to their continuing interest in the EPs and the London Marathon that all those contacted have been keen to participate in the research. They have all provided extraordinary, amusing and poignant stories.

Of these twenty seven non active EPs ten completed the research survey and were subsequently followed up with phone calls in providing additional background detail for their biographies. The remaining seventeen could not be contacted but with the cooperation of the running magazine, Athletics Weekly three more agreed to participate, totalling thirteen. Subsequently, the final overall sample of 66% (27) for active and inactive Eps was well in excess of the initial target of 50%.

The EPs will be listed in the order of the year that they became inactive, and those that contributed to the research are * asterisked.

All the biographical information for the non-contributors has been taken from the EPs website www.everpresent.org.uk. and logs their marathon times (fastest and slowest), club affiliation and the year they became non-active.

DR. HAROLD CHADWICK   1996
2:24:10

Harold Chadwick of Bournemouth AC and the Thames Hare & Hounds was an EP for one year only. He was the first EP to DNF (did not finish) after his 16th London, the year after EP recognition. His time in the year he dropped out, 1996, was 4:19:31. Ironically, Dr. Harold was the fastest EP in 1981 with a scorching 2:24:10. What a pity he didn't continue!

* BRYAN READ 1998 2:45:00

Bryan Read of Orion Harriers and Walthamstow AC had a time of 3:34:05 for the inaugural London and after 18 Londons his time of 3:52:36 in 1998, showed an amazingly consistent sequence of times. His fastest recorded London was 2:45:00 in 1987.

Among his total marathon haul of 25 in the UK and New York, he ran the Windsor Poly Marathon four times with a fast finish in the 1983 event of 2:56 for 3rd place. In similar vein Bryan also ran the Harlow Marathon a few times and in 1983 finished 3rd overall in a very quick time of 2:40.

A truly memorable occasion for him in the Harlow Marathon was to be presented with his Essex Championships medal by the legendary marathoner Jim Peters. Another special memory was in an inter-club 5 mile relay race at Haringey when running against Seb Coe. *"I stayed with him for about 200 yards"* Bryan lamented.

His most enjoyable marathon was the 1984 London, not only because he ran faster than expected in 2:40 but finished just behind the top woman marathoner Lesley Watson! In London 1987 he was 1st O/45 and the next year as his reward proudly wore the V1 vest

Severe knee arthritis in 1998 was the cause of his worst marathon experience and his last London when he struggled to finish in 3:52:36. This condition worsened in 1999 and lead to his having a complete knee replacement. The loss of his active EP status in 1999 was a real blow to Bryan as he saw his regular Londons each year as *"a major part of my life that all my training was built around."*

Before taking up serious running, Bryan was a budding football star captaining England's under 13's against Scotland and remembers a taxi ride to one of the matches with England's greatest footballer Bobby Moore.

Presently, he keeps fit training with the local triathletes in Hackney with 3k swims, three times a week. That's a two mile swim!

* ALASTAIR AITKEN   1999   2:47:58

A Highgate Harriers stalwart, Alastair Aitken ran the first London in a quick sub 3 hour of 2:53:01 and improved on his time in 1982 with his fastest marathon of 2:47:58.   Alastair's marathon total of 21, is two more than his Londons which he loved *"especially when running around the Cutty Sark (at 7 miles) and feeling really relaxed, before the pain set in!"*

On non marathon runs, in his thirties and forties, he remembers *"delightful runs around Virginia Water (Surrey), Longcross, and around Blenheim Park, the*

Duke of Marlborough seat before breakfast when residing at the Bear Inn near Woodstock – wonderful memories!" Ah, just some of the joys of running.

Unfortunately Alastair had to relinquish his EP status just three days before the 20th London in 1999 when he was hit by a motorcycle, suffering many serious broken bones and fractures. Bad luck or what!

GEOFFREY BALFOUR   2000   2:30:48

Geoff Balfour of Huncote Harriers was a sub 3 hour runner with a first London time of 2:45:00 and his fastest in 1984 in 2:30:48. In fact he ran the first six Londons under 3 hours finishing as an EP after twenty circuits in 2001 with a 3:43:41 age 50.

REGINALD BROWN   2000   3:07:38

Reg Brown of South London Harriers had a first London in a very respectable 3:07:38 when 49 years old and after 20 Londons his time of 6:29:41 was a little more modest.

JOHN LEGGE   2000 RIP   3:02:35

John Legge, the ex President of Orion Harriers started his London runs with his fastest London in 3:02:35 and ended with a 4:52:09 in 2000, his slowest.

John had been busy as usual at the club when he was suddenly taken ill and died. Mike Peel received the following message from his club colleague Roddy MacLennan.

This message was received on 19 February 2001

'Hi Mike.

I know you were recently in touch with John our ex-president - and one of the Everpresents at the London marathon.
John died on Sunday morning. He had been up at the club marshalling our club championship, helping with the timekeeping and in the pub afterwards - full of wit and humour. Quite a shock. He's already missed.'
All the best Roddy MacLennan @ Orion

* **ERIK FALCK-THERKELSEN** 2001   2:45:33

Erik Falck-Therkelsen of Woking AC was 40 years old when running his first London and gauged it to perfection by achieving a sub 3 hour time, by one second in 2:59:59 – phew!   After his sterling efforts his *'changing room'* was behind a double sewn bath towel at the rear of Buckingham Palace!   This finish time became the start of a run of sub 3 hour marathons with ten in the first eleven years, culminating in his fastest of 2:45:33.

Unfortunately he ended his EP tenure after 21 Londons at the tender age of 60 in a time of 3:35:03 and only 35 minutes slowest than his first. He did however run four more Londons after 2002 ending with a very respectable 4:02 in 2006, *"but the enjoyment was fading"* he said.

Erik was shocked before the 1984 London when he received a rejection, but decided to run anyway under the name of another runner.   Eventually with the help of John Legge, another EP. Erik was reinstated under the *'fast for age'* rule.

He has now completed 48 marathons in the UK and worldwide but non in his home country of Norway. Erik counts the 1987 London as one of his most enjoyable in winning a sponsored £20 for his charity by finishing under 2:48 by just ten seconds; close!

Erik's first marathon in the mid 1970's was the tough Masters & Maidens Marathon with 2,000 feet of climb, a run he was thoughtfully *"recommended"* by the Club's discus coach. His time of 3:07:08 for a first marathon was brilliant!   In the race he accidentally knocked over a cyclist and runner who was being paced, but after a few choice *'words'* they continued as buddies.

Erik had taken up running primarily to keeps fit having joined the City of London Polytechnic gym club for circuit training.   He was then inspired by the runners at Woking AC to enter the monthly handicap races after which long distance running took hold.

Erik then graduated into ultra marathon runs. One of which was the mid-summer South Downs Way, a tortuous and undulating distance of 80 miles. He ran this in a best time of 11:26 and was first in his age group (50 – 55) in 1993   He ran it ten times in all, an exceptional feat!   Another ultra favourite of Erik's was the Punchbowl Marathon in Surrey, a trail and cross country event of 33 miles organised by the LDWA (Long Distance Walkers Association) with his fastest, a very quick time of 5:04.

In his teenage years in Norway Erik competed as a ski jumper and coupled that with cross country skiing, Norway's most popular sport and his favourite means of getting to school.   He is still a very keen walker having *'knocked off'* all the Wainwright walks along with heavy duty walks such as the Cumbria Way, the Offas Dyke Path and the Ridgeway Path.

Finally in 2005 he completed the S.W.Coast Path from Minehead to Poole in 3-5 day blocks.   It only took him three years!   Erik hopes to restart some gentle 3 to 6 mile runs just as soon as he has recovered from a double rupture to his quads.   Good luck Erik!

CHRISTOPHER ADAMS 2002 **RIP**   2:48:14

Chris Adams ran for Orion Harriers and was a serious sub 3 hour man running his first London in 2:49:37 at the youthful age of 38.   He ran nine of the first 10 Londons in under three hours with a fastest time of 2:48:14 in 1987 when he was 44.

His last London in 2002 was a very respectable 3:29:03 but later that year Chris died on the 31st October 2002 aged only 59.

MAX JONES 2002 **RIP** 2:58:08

Max Jones of Birchfield Harriers in Birmingham ran his first London in 3:51:52 at the relatively mature age of 53 and was the 2nd oldest EP, to Reg Burbidge. Max ran two of his sub 3 hour Londons, his fastest in 1983 in 2:58:08 and in 1986 a 2:59:54. This nerve jangling sub 3 hour run was completed at the ripe old age, for a marathoner, of 58!

His slowest in London 2000 was 6:17:04, at the age of 72 then just failing to make the 2003 after completing 22 Londons. Sadly, Max died on the 14th March 2010 age 83. The following message was sent by his family.

This message was received by Mike Peel on 15 March 2010

"You will have known my father as a family friend, as a participant in (the) London Marathon, and on The Walk most years, as a helper at elections, as a spectator at football matches or in many other ways.

Katy and I need to tell you that he died yesterday. He had a fall at home in Leeds on Saturday night which caused a series of brain haemorrhages. He died in Leeds General Infirmary. Katy, Matthew and I were at his bedside along with my mother & sister and many other close family and friends.

It is very sad to know how fit and healthy he was, even at the age of 83, so such a shock to know that he is no longer with us, and so suddenly. But we are happy that he died surrounded by family and friends, as peacefully as these things are, and without a prolonged illness which after his active life he would not have endured."

Born June 3rd, 1927 Died 14th March 2010

As a mark of Max's commitment and contribution to running, the following record is surely a testimony to his long term running prowess, world records and self deprecating humour. Some highlights that follow are from his running log.

'1943 June: Ran 1 mile, aged just 16, in 5:03.4 on virtually no training.
1946 Dec : for Cambridge University v Oxford. 7½ miles X-Country : 1st me; **2nd Roger Bannister**
1989 April : 1st Senior (over 60) 92nd Boston Marathon (USA) in 3:03:46 and 5th M60, 6 days later, in London, in 3:09:29.
1995 July Silver medallist, individual and team, M65 marathon, WAVA World Championships, in Buffalo, NY, United States.
1997 Aug : gained all the M70 track ultra WRs 100km (10:31:31), through 100 miles in (18:16:47) to

24hrs (191.019km, i.e. 118 miles 1220 yards) and finished 2nd overall in the race, my highest position for 49 years! September - ran M70 WRs for 50km (4:16:12); 40 miles (5:49:50); 50 miles (7:34:32).

Certainly Max was one of the EP characters par excellence!

LIONEL MANN   2002   2:57:12

Lionel Mann of Belgrave Harriers had a sub 3 hour London to his credit in 1985 with a time of 2:57:12 age 44 and also his fastest. He then proceeded to run 22 Londons until retiring with a time of 6:07:32 when a relatively youthful 61. In 2003 he started but unfortunately did not finish his 23rd London.

MICHAEL STAR   2002   2:43:26

Mike Starr of St. Albans Striders finished his 1981 London with a purposeful 3:37:11 and then proceeded to run the next 11 out of 14 Londons under the 3 hour mark, the only blip was an uncharacteristic 4:54:39 in 1988. His fastest of 2:43:26 came in 1985. Mike eventually ended his EP run in 2002 with a 3:48:46, aged a young 58.

*** MICK McGEOCH** 2000 2:17:58

Only nine seconds separated Mick McGeoch of Les Croupiers from being the fastest EP in 1981 in a blistering time of 2:24:19 and 58th overall in the inaugural London. This was some achievement with over 7,700 odd starters. His time was well and truly eclipsed in 1983 in a phenomenal 2:17:58 for his fastest. In fact, right up until he had a DNS (did not start) for the 2003 London he ran 22 sub 3 hour marathons, his last only 12 minutes slower than his first in 2:36:20 for his 22$^{nd.}$ This is high level consistent elite running by any standards.

Fig 2. Mick McGeoch's 22 Charted times .

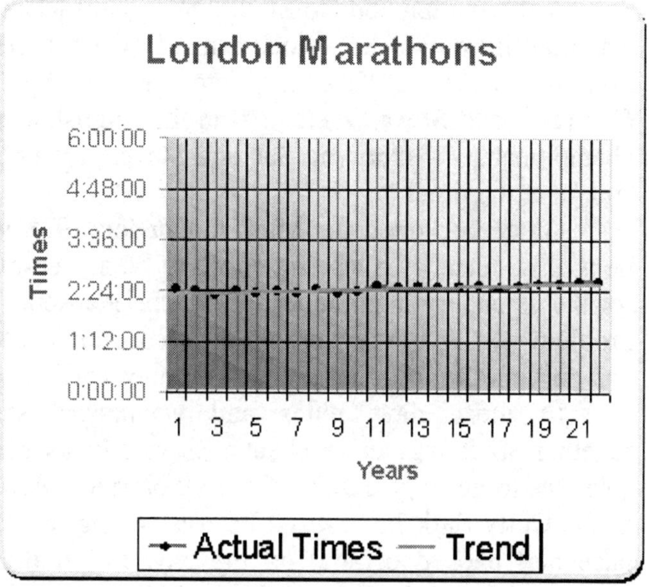

The chart shows how little Mick's times have changed over his 22 Marathons, almost a flatline!

After his DNS in 2003 resulting from a severe achilles injury in the 10 mile Ballycotton race, Mick returned to complete another seven Londons to clock up an impressive 27 in total.

Mick's marathon times make for mouth-watering reading for a number of reasons. He has run two sub 2:20's, and 40, **yes 40**. sub 2:30 marathons. In addition he has won four UK marathons all of them in sub 2:30 times. The Heart of England 1984, in 2:22:07; the

Polytechnic Windsor 1987; in 2:28:49; the Abingdon 1988, in 2:24:49 and the St. Albans 1990, in 2:24:24.

A fascinating coda to Mick's St. Albans Marathon was that the runner he shaded into 2nd place, a certain Finn by the name of Kira Dumbleton actually beat **Seb Coe** (10th) and **Steve Ovett** (2nd) in the English schools championships - mind you Seb and Steve were only 15 and 16 at the time!

Glory beckoned for Mick in London 1988 when he was targeted by a leading coach to be a pace-maker for the legendary marathoner Ingrid Christiansen. The problem was that they were on different start lines and had only met for the first time ten minutes earlier.

In those days elites and wannabees started together so it was quite chaotic especially as Mick's role was to get Ingrid under the 2:20 barrier. Arriving at the Cutty Sark he realised he was setting too fast a pace and backed off but on the day, Ingrid did not perform to her potential and finished in a disappointing 2:25:42.

Of all the 75 marathons that Mick started only three ended in DNF's, a truly impressive record.

His shorter races are just as spectacular with 24:33 for 5 miles; 49:18 for 10 and a truly speedy half marathon at Rhymny, Wales in 66:15. On the track he is no slouch either, winning the 1997 5,000 metres British Masters title in a time of 15:26. Even Mo Farah would have been impressed with his 64 second last lap! A running friend, Archie Jenkins came 3rd behind Mick and gave him a video of the race as a memento. When he needs cheering up Mick says he sits down with a beer and watches a re-run of the race!

Mick is still a youthful 58 and says his running saga started in 1980 with twelve runners who split from the Cardiff club to form their own. *Les Croupiers* was named after the local casino owner Gordon MacIlroy, who sponsored their kit.

His most enjoyable marathon was in the AAA Championships in 1983 when he left the field trailing, in a time of 2:17:58. His worst marathon experience by far was missing the 2003 London. Deciding to support the runners on the course at the fifteen mile mark he called out to his friend Chris Finill, who immediately ran over and gave him a big hug. Mick recalls *"I just burst out crying, with tears running down my face!"*

* PETER GREENWOOD   2002   2:37:18

Peter Greenwood has the doubtful distinction of being the only EP to drop out in 2003 with a DNF (did not finish), having completed 22 Londons. He ran for Canterbury Harriers AC and managed a sub 3 hour for his first London in 2:46.53 age 38. His best London was two years later in a speedy 2:42:52.

Peter has run the prodigious total of 176 marathons all around the world. The one marathon he DNF (did not finish) was the Flying Fox Marathon which he put down to the wrong shoes!!!? Pardon?

Cliff Temple the Times sports reporter gave him an amusing marathon quote when he said *"sex before the marathon is OK, as long as you don't block the road!"* Peter finally finished with a 5:27:56 in his final year still a youthful 59.

DERICK FISHER   2004   2:52:44

Derrick Fisher of Newport Harriers was a mature 45 for his first London and like many other quality EPs managed a sub 3 hour in 2:56:22. His fastest London was three years later in 1984 with an improved 2:52:44. Derrick's last London time slipped to 5:43:30 but only after 24 Londons. Another creditable long haul.

DON MARTIN   2005   4:10:00

Don Martin ran for the Royal Parks Police in 1981 for his first and fastest London in 4:10:00 and after 25 Londons he retired as an EP with a time of 6:39:08, aged 64.

* JAN HILDRETH   2005   2:54:13

Jan Hildreth, a runner for the prestigious Thames Hare & Hounds club ran his first London in a fine 3:25:37 as a mature 48 year old but wondered if his first London in 1981 was destined to be his last? It wasn't by a long chalk. After another three Londons he had his fastest with a 2:54:13 in 1985 and ran more than one London with the author John Bryant, a good friend and member of the Thames club.

Twenty five years later he bowed out as an EP with a 6:16:08 in 2005 and his slowest London when he cramped up badly in the latter stages, partly due to serious spinal problems.

Jan was also a keen orienteer for many years, competing in the Karrimor Mountain Marathon, a gruelling annual two day event with a wilderness stopover, necessitating the paired runners to carry all their two day supplies and equipment. For additional recreation Jan was a keen cross country skier, regularly visiting the French alps each winter.

Jan is now 71 and in poor health but remembers being an EP and competing in his 25 Londons as *"lots of fun"*.

* PETER SHEPHEARD   2005   2:28:16

Peter Shepheard is another Scottish born EP who decamped to Bromley in Kent and joined the famous Blackheath Harriers who were one of the first clubs to provide marshals for the early Londons. With twenty five Londons under his belt and a very speedy 2:28:16 for his fastest, he was only two minutes behind Grete Waitz the female winner in 1983.

Peter maintained a remarkably consistent performance for the first nine Londons when he ran well under 3 hours. This surely confirmed that making a start at fifteen, as he did at Wallasey Grammar paid off in the long run.

His inspiration at the time was the 1950's working class hero Alf Tupper in The Rover comic series *'The Tough of the Track'*. *Alf* trained on fish and chips and ran in old plimsolls but always beat the *'toffs'*. Chris Chataway and Gordon Pirie were his real life role models that he would watch in local National Cross Country races.

Although Peter has raced abroad in shorter runs his total of 40 marathons have been mainly in the South of England i.e. The Polytechnic, Plymouth, Maidstone and Harlow marathons, when he ran with the iconic Peter Thompson.

He vividly remembers running the first London in a March downpour and after a very brisk start was told by a friend in the crowd he was in the first fifty. He eventually finished close to Joyce Smith the first female winner of London, in a time of 2:29:47. Peter was in a 200 yard dash to the finish with fifty other runners and later that day saw himself on the BBC TV summary and said *"this was about the only time I have appeared on the small screen."*

Around this time, he started training for the Milton Keynes Olympic Trials Marathon but could not compete for six months due to an injured back.

Over the years Peter has suffered a veritable catalogue of mishaps during his runs. Bitten by dogs, beaten up by dog owners, tripping over loose paving slabs and suffering a fracture of the fibula, but through all of these set-backs and more he kept going to remain an EP.

His 1983 London is remembered for two conflicting reasons. Being pushed into the 3 hour enclosure and taking 20 minutes to run the first three miles then, with only two miles to go running along the Embankment and zipping past Ron Hill the running addict of the decade, to finish in 2:28:16 and his fastest.

Peter almost missed the 1993 London after an Alsatian knocked him over on a park training run to leave him badly bruised with breathing and eyesight problems, later diagnosed as a torn heart ventricle. Having the EPs mentality he still completed the 1993 and 1994 marathons in just over 3 hours!

Peter's marathon build-up mileage for these runs was a weekly total of 90 for 30 weeks, totalling 2,700 miles! Outside the marathon it would dip to 60 weekly miles. No wonder he expected fast times in the marathon with this intensive training and got annoyed when denied a clear run at the start!

In 2004 he barely made the start line due to a snarl up near Blackheath but his wife came to his aid with a well timed lift. Resulting from this near squeak he left home for the 2005 marathon at 5 a.m. but suffered in the cold for 3 hours and struggled to finish in 6:05:50.

"It got worse in 2006" Peter said when he was finally forced to throw in the towel by the rash actions of a careless young lady runner whom he tried to avoid near the Cutty Sark, tearing a hamstring in the process and then limping out a mile later around the eight mile mark.

Peter's critique on aspects of the marathon are certainly borne of his experiences. 1. Because of the various start times roads were closed too early forcing runners to start out earlier and earlier. 2. The celebrity culture changed the marathon into a glorified charity run with the result that good club runners were blocked and their running times suffered. 3. Foreign runners were given priority in Greenwich Park which had the effect of blocking good club runners. 4. Wheelchair racers which started with the main field were a nightmare because downhill they could reach speeds well in excess of the fastest runners. Even now elite wheelchairs are not isolated sufficiently from either elite runners or the masses it is argued. Mick McGeoch made similar comments about the erosion of marathon times. Wheelchair issues made the news again in the 2013 marathon with a collition at a drinks station.between an elite wheelchair athlete and an elite woman.

Peter's shorter runs and cross country races have also been pretty quick with a half marathon in 1:08. He even shaded Dave Bedford by two minutes in the

Shaftesbury 10 mile back in the 1960's. His most enjoyable runs were the cross country *'mob matches'* when Blackheath competed against three other top London clubs.

He is no slouch at other sports; playing football until aged 60 and in earlier years, triathlons and bike time-trials.

* **RAYMOND JOHNSON** 2006   3:01:58

Until 2006 Ray Johnson of Kimberley & District Striders (Nottingham) was an EP stalwart. His first London was completed in a speedy 3:11:00 but his fastest, just missing out on a sub 3 was 3:01:58 in 1989 at the mature age of 56 – some going! Imagine his times if he had started running earlier?

After 27 consecutive marathons, Ray's London EP saga ended in 2008 by gout in his knee. Ray said that he did not run that year due to pleas from his family and doctor and said *"it still hurts to see the EP list of finishers every year"*. His comment clearly shows how much EP status meant and this is born out by his 1982 London when he ran with a fractured cheek bone suffered in a football match only two weeks before. He still ran a quickish 3:17:15! After losing his EP status Ray returned to run the following year and said *"it was OK"*.

Ray has now run 50 marathons in the UK and overseas, one of the toughest being the Snowdon Marathon in 1990. You don't actually run **up** Snowdon but the undulating route is tough, really tough, with a 4 mile sting in the tale at about the 22 mile mark.

Thirty years ago Ray's employers, the Nottingham Fire Service's running team was his inspiration for the first London. He is now 80 but still runs regularly and has entered the Robin Hood half Marathon this year. What an example to the younger generation.

* REGINALD BURBIDGE   2007   3:42:03

Reg Burbidge of Highgate Harriers has the distinction of being our oldest EP at 88. He completed 27 Londons and 30 marathons overall with his fastest in the 1983 London of 3:42:03.

His most enjoyable was the first London which he said, as his first competitive marathon, *"gave him. 'goosebumps' with the anticipation of participating in a world event"*. It was a double-whammy for Reg. because he achieved his target with a sub 4 hour time.

His worst marathon was when he decided to follow a serious walker who was weaving his way through packs of runners and eventually was out of sight, leaving Reg with one of his slowest times and totally deflated. *"Lesson learned"* Reg. said! *"Always go at your own pace"*. Very sound advice.

He also remembers a burning hot London when the water stations ran out and he had to raid the Special Drinks stations (for elite runners) for a drink which was, very sweet, cloying and did nothing to quench his thirst. It did however give him an incentive to get to the finish quicker!

Reg. was also featured in the 2005 London Marathon magazine as *'the oldest of the EPs (at 80)'* having run his first at 54 when he used to run 30-40 miles a week and has never owned a car. *"The marathon is tortuous but it's something to achieve. My target is to keeps going probably for around six hours. It's not a race, only the youngsters think that".* Reg. concluded.

In his final London in 2007 he finished in a time of 6:53:27, not bad for an 80 year old. His take on being an EP is *"It's a fraternity: no-one wants to see anyone drop out"*

* MIKE WILKINSON   2007   2:45:00

Mike Wilkinson creator of the Duke Street Runners also ran for Norwich City AC, his home town club, and is a sub 3 hour man with a best time of

2:49:42 in London 1984. He is also one of our ultra-marathon heroes with four 24 hour races under his belt and one clocked at 117 miles! Next up was a 100k race in 10:30 and with a whopping total of over 150 marathons to his credit he must have stamina with a capital 'S'.

N.B. In the 1981 London he wanted to finish in the first 1,000 and guess where he finished? 1,000th!

The 1981 inaugural is memorable for the *"lousy weather; sleet and snow."* He was accompanied by his wife Eileen and two youngest sons Andrew and Christopher with their Springer Spaniel Harvey on a lead. As a warm up before the start the runners received a steaming mug of Bovril and although Mike missed out on the hot drink, he found a discarded mug which he still keeps as a memento!

His best marathon was the Windsor which he remembers as a nice course, running free on a sunny, summers day in the 1980's and coming in at around 3 hours. Mike's worst was his local Norfolk Marathon where he was also the course organiser, and ran it six days after a 24 hour race; not a good decision as he pulled out after 23 miles.

In 1982, Mike ran the 1st. Norfolk Marathon in 3:00:25 and on the following Sunday the London Marathon in 3:12:35, just to prove that running 26.2 is no big deal. Spoken like a true ultra!

Mike is no *'also-ran'* in the shorter distances either, combining stamina and strength with speed. Here is just a selection of his times, starting from short to long runs on the track. 400 m in 56 seconds; 1:58

for a ½ mile; 4:18 for a mile and 1:14 for a ½ marathon – these are seriously quick times .

He started running Mike said *"at ten because I couldn't get to school on time",* and basically never stopped!

During the 2007 London he consumed 12 paracetamol whereupon he passed out, was attended to by the St. John's team and finished in a pedestrian 6:53:20 but can't remember much about it. Maybe all these 24 hour runs and arthritic toes account for his DNS in 2008 and put paid to his EP status? Nevertheless he did complete 27 Londons and is always there for our pre-race photo, come rain or shine. Mike is real credit to the EP fraternity.

JOHN HANSCOMBE 2008 2:49:19

John Hanscombe of Ranelagh Harriers ran the first London in 2:54:29. His fastest was in 1983 with a quick 2:49:19 and for the first six Londons was under the 3 hour mark. John's last, in 2008 was in 4:46:37, still a pretty good time for a 72 year old.

He eventually bowed out in his 29th London with a DNF, apparently getting to the halfway mark but we don't know why. Was it accident, injury, illness or something else?

* ROGER MAWER 2009   2:40:00

Roger Mawer ran for Lowestoft RR where he is a life member and for his first London finished in a quick sub 3 hour 2:58:04. His fastest was in the Southend Marathon in a fast 2:40. Roger has now completed 55 marathons plus shorter runs all over the world. On these shorter runs of the ½ marathon (1:15) and 10 mile (55 mins) he is equally as speedy.

Roger's impressive CV shows that thirteen of his first fourteen Londons were completed in under the 3 hour mark, the last of which was a 2:55:12 in 2004.

He says his most enjoyable marathon was in Barnsley which he called '*The Beast*' complete with three hills, in the early 1980's. On the way his friend asked a pub customer for a quaff of his beer, took the tankard and kept on running, much to the customers chagrin. Well, it was in a jolly good cause!

On the flip side, his worst marathon was his last London in 2009. He had been in and out of hospital with physio treatment for his legs and in the marathon he felt quite ill and although suffering from depression still managed to finish in 5:20.41. It was to be his last Marathon as an EP. Roger completed 29 consecutive Londons and narrowly failed to finish in 2010 when he suffered serious leg cramps at 18 miles with just eight miles to go.

He is also a dab hand at dingy sailing, winning lots of trophies at the Stokes Bay Sailing Club near Portsmouth and was short-listed in the 3 man dingy lightweight crew for the Mexico Olympics in 1968. Obviously an all-round athlete of some standing.

Being an EP he says has meant a lot to him in making him "*lots of friends all around the world.*"

* DAVID CLARK   2010   2:41:56

Newbury AC's Dave Clark is another ultra runner with the London to Brighton under his belt for a club record of 7:10.

In his 3rd London he set his fastest marathon of all in a time of 2:41:56 and for the first 12 Londons Dave ran ten of them in under 3 hours, some feat! He even surprised himself in the race by running a negative split (faster 2nd half) and said *"it was most enjoyable"*. Running along the Victoria Embankment at about 25 miles he caught Lesley Watson, one of our top women marathoners, then at Westminster Bridge he eased past her to finish well ahead.   Lesley would not have been amused!

Dave nearly missed one London when the Club minibus punctured and they could not change the wheel despite using a scaffold pole for extra leverage. *"Fortunately we eventually found out that Ford Transit nuts unscrewed clockwise and just got there in time"* said Dave.

At 39, he was a late starter to running in the mid 1970's.   Dave wanted to lose some of his 14 stones so he joined the jogging section of his club and started with 3 mile fun runs then, graduating to longer races he quickly shed the weight down to 10 stone.   Dave was on his way!

He also recalls a risqué story involving the first London's basic changing facilities on the baggage buses. While helping a young lady runner preserve her modesty with a well placed towel, the true *'gentlemen'* still took a quick peek.   Very naughty!

His slowest London was 5:45:55 in 2007 and this was a blip because Dave actually got faster after that and ended his EP status in 2010 with a 5:18:49 age 74.

He had aimed to complete 30 Londons and although he would have liked to continue, the training needed to keep in trim was getting too hard.   His eventual total of 45 completed marathons were run all over the UK   Being an EP, Dave said *"was like wearing a special badge, it was never going to get any better or bigger"*

DERRICK PICKERING *2010*   *2:36:29*
Derrick Pickering of East Hull Harriers AC ran his first London in a fast time of 2:38:38 and his final one in 2010 in 5:12:53 aged 74.. With a total of 72 marathons his fastest was in the 1983 London with an elite time of 2:36:29.

* RAINER BURCHETT 2011   2:57:26
What commitment Rainer Burchett of Shaftesbury Barnet Harriers and Keswick AC has with 31 London marathons, narrowly missing out through injury for his 32nd in 2012. Just think of the training miles Rainer has racked up to achieve his best marathon in a sub 3 hour 2:57:26.

He tells a curious story a year before London in 1981 when he ran the Masters & Maidens Marathon over the Hog's Back in Surrey in 3:00:51, coming 7th O/40. At the time Rainer says it was one of the biggest road races in the UK with 800 runners. Twenty five years later he unearthed the race results to find out that *"only a couple of minutes ahead of me in 4th place', was one of* the *current EPs, Pat Dobbs"* Small world Rainer!

His worst marathon was hitting *'the wall'* after only 2 miles in 1996; is this a record for an EP? It was however, only six days after running the 100th Boston in a time of 3:20. Rainer's time of 3:38 in London the following week was his slowest to date but still pretty respectable. London 2011 eclipsed that when Rainer *'ran'* with a leg brace, finishing in 7:15:07 and the slowest ever EP! Rainer joked *"I would have been faster but peanut butter and cucumber sandwiches supplied by friends, slowed me down!"* Despite all the agony, EPs still retain a sense of humour

But running is not his only sporting interest with recreational tennis, black run skiing and scuba diving filling the sporting gaps. One of his most recent events at the ripe old age of 70 was to complete the Ross Naylor Challenge which involved a distance of 48 miles, 18,000 feet of climb while scaling 30 peaks in a M70 record time of 18:15. What an achievement! Interestingly, the event was dreamed up by one Chris Brasher in 1990.

When at Cambridge he coxed for his College boat and afterwards played competitive tennis at Globe LTC.

TONY TILLBROOKE 2011 2:44:22

Tony Tillbrooke of Victory AC ran his first London as a mature forty-one year old in 3:42:24 but improved his times dramatically in the next five Londons to post a best marathon time of 2:44:22 in 1986. His final and 31st London was timerd at 6:42:59 when far from his best.

Unfortunately, Tony could not be contacted after the 2012 marathon when he was 72, despite many attempts. It is assumed that he was more likely to have been a DNS as no-one saw him before the 2012 start.

* MICHAEL PEEL 2012   2:40:30

Another speedy marathoner is Mike Peel. A member and former Past President of Blackheath & Bromley Harriers now age 71, had a quick time of 2:40:30 in his first London and was 7th fastest out of the original 42.

One of his *'slowest'* marathons, a 4:15:35 in 1984 was due to escorting Alan Pickering, a blind runner all the way! Mike has been inside 3 hours on twenty four occasions and *'thinks'* his first marathon was in the 1978 Harlow in a truly remarkable time for a *'virgin'* of

2:44:44. Wait a minute, who doesn't clearly remember the fine detail of their first marathon?

Was his *"most enjoyable marathon"* a 2:46:44. on the Isle of Wight because of the attractive scenery or was it because he was near the top of the veterans standings? His worst marathon experience was in 1996 when he developed a serious dose of calf cramp at the Cutty Sark after 7 miles and had to walk most of the concluding nineteen miles, ending in a time of 4:50:43. Mind you, he had the excuse of having run the Boston Centenary Marathon only six days earlier!

Ultra distances do not faze Mike either because in a London Marathon year he ran a very sprightly London to Brighton (*54 miles 856 yards Mike says*) in 7:03:29. His shorter distance times are equally speedy with 53.0 for 400 metres and a fast 55:30 for 10 miles.

Including his Londons, Mike has run '*about 60'* marathons mainly in the UK. Another noteworthy experience for Mike was on one of his training runs when he accompanied the London Marathon creator, Chris Brasher of Ranelagh Harriers but *"only for a while"*. Why, was he or Chris too fast?

Along with most other EPs Mike has a few other activities in his sports CV locker. A keen walker, climbing Mount Kilimanjaro a few years ago, a black run skier for many years and still a competitive member and Past President of his cycling club De Laune CC.

All the EPs were dismayed when they learned that due to a debilitating illness Mike had to relinquish his EP status in 2013 after 32 Londons. He did at least start the 33rd with the comment. *"I'd rather be a DNF (did not finish) than a DNS (did not start)"* Despite this, Mike will still oversee our Everpresents website, a decision the EPs as a whole heartily welcomed.

Webmaster's Postscript
Mike posted the reasons for his EPs swansong on the Everpresents website.

"I am sorry to tell you but my Ever-Present status for the London Marathon has come to an end. I have been unwell since my last run on 17 March (2013) and have not run a step since and can just about walk to the local shops.

I'm receiving treatment albeit with little effect and the Doctors and my family have advised me that it would be foolish to even attempt the (Marathon) event. All being well I hope to be at the registration on Thursday and at the photo call on Sunday, my last as an active EP.

My intention, at the moment, is to attempt to start the race, do 100 yards and then drop out. I feel I would rather be a DNFer (did not finish) than a DNSer (did not start)! Only you will understand why.

So, 32 Londons and carrying the Olympic Relay Torch is not too bad for an old man to bow out on, and all good things come to an end after all! Thank you all for your support over the years and especially to my family and Terri."

Fig. 3 Ever-presents Remaining by Year

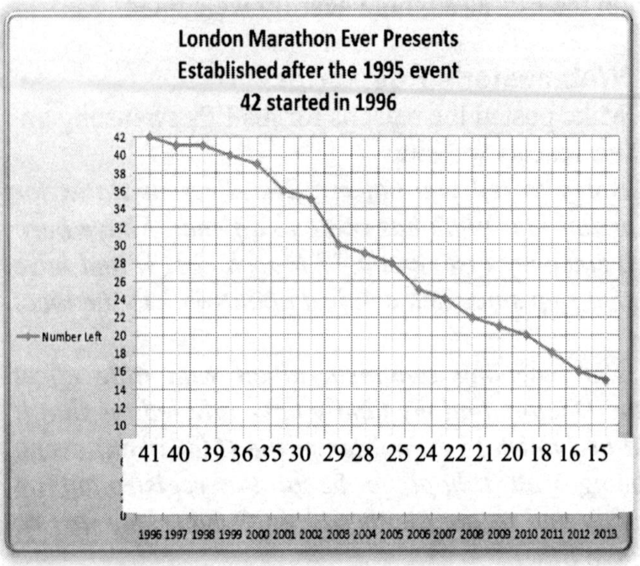

London Marathon Ever Presents
Established after the 1995 event
42 started in 1996

41 40 39 36 35 30 29 28 25 24 22 21 20 18 16 15

1996 1997 1998 1999 2000 2001 2002 2003 2004 2005 2006 2007 2008 2009 2010 2011 2012 2013

LIST OF EPs BY YEAR OF LEAVING.

Below are the names of the EPs and their year of departure from the London.

HAROLD CHADWICK 1996; BRYAN READ 1998; ALASTAIR AITKEN 1999;

REG. BROWN 2000; GEOFF BALFOUR 2000; ERIK FALK-THERKELSEN 2001;

JOHN LEGGE 2001 RIP; MAX JONES 2002 RIP; LIONEL MANN 2002;

MICHAEL STAR 2002; MICK MCGEOCH 2002; PETER GREENWOOD 2002;

CHRIS ADAMS 2002 RIP; DERECK FISHER 2004; DON MARTIN 2005;

PETER SHEPSHEARD 2005; JAN HILDRETH 2005; RAY JOHNSON 2006;

REG. BURBIDGE 2007; JOHN HASCOMBE 2008; MIKE WILKINSON 2008;
ROGER MAWER 2009; DERECK PICKERING 2010; DAVE CLARK 2010;
RAINER BURCHETT 2011; TONY TILLBROOKE 2012 MIKE PEEL 2012;

Over the years the EPs have fallen by the wayside at an average of 1.5 annually with 2006 being the exception, when there were no casualties. The largest annual fallout was in 2002 with six EPs, four times the normal wastage but despite that blip **Fig.3.** above shows a fairly even drop-out over the years.

A mark of distinction for the EPs as a group, was that four were nominated to represent Great Britain in the Olympic Torch Relay in 2012. i.e. Messrs. Gordon, Jones, Peel and O'Connor. This was in large part due to their having run every London Marathon and the recognition by the selectors of the extraordinary talent, determination and dedication that being an EP demands.

Distance preferences.

Many EPs have found their running preferences in races of widely differing distances and places. They rarely stick to one distance because each supplies a particular training need or personal desire. Some prefer a mix of short speed events up to ½ marathon, leading to a marathon while others need a challenge to push their bodies to the limit in ultra events such as 100k, 24 hour, 40 mile, double marathons or even ***Ironman** triathlons.

Two EPs have taken the ultimate challenge of running across the USA. Others have travelled the world in search of the best marathon or perhaps they were just footloose.

* **Ironman distances** 2.4 mile swim, 112 mile bike, 26.2 mile run.

John Bryant's   Ever-present marathon jottings

As a footnote to this section of the book, the thoughts and comments of various EPs through the writings of John Bryant, in his book 'The London Marathon' is worth quoting.

Bryant recalls that Jan Hildreth, (2005) a close friend and running colleague commented on training in the streets. *"Years ago, if you ran the streets to keep fit you ran the gauntlet of schoolboy taunts and abuse – the London changed all that; we are no longer eccentrics, we're heroes, setting out on this odyssey year after year".*

Dave Clark (2010) thinks that running 25 marathons *"is no great achievement but running 25 consecutive Londons has been a problem for most of us, running with illness and injury. I've ran with stress fractures, fractured ribs, strained muscles and flu just to keeps up the sequence, because it was the London."*

In underlining this dedication to go through hell and high water in keeping up the sequence, Bryant uses Don Martin (2005) as an example, *"he is addicted to running the London. He's run with a broken toe, a crippled back and a wrecked knee."* Don concludes, *"I suppose it's stupidity that keeps me going, but I love it for all the crowds and getting over the line. To run down the Mall and finish is very emotional and the most wonderful feeling."*

Finally, Jeff Gordon believes *"people only take notice of you if you've run the London even if you've finished high up in other marathons; nobody cares. They are only impressed if you have actually finished the London."*

The thoughts of these four EPs are in a real sense the *raison d'etre* of all the EPs active or inactive, in that the London is a truly special marathon and that being part of the EPs is something unique.

Chapter 4 Summary

The participating 27 EP's have run a total of 1,727 marathons but improbably there is an almost even split between the active EPs (863) and the non-active EPs (864), a truly surprising statistic. Of course it should be remembered that this statistic is based on 27 and not the 39 EP tota'. Since 1996 when the EPs were formed 27 have dropped out for a variety of reasons, none voluntarily it must be said, and all were greatly saddened to miss the camaraderie, buzz and the occasion of being on the start line each year.

How many will start the 2014 London or even finish remains to be seen but it is clear that those who do drop out, if indeed any do, will not go without a fight, based on the evidence of the preceding biographies.

EVER-PRESENTS MEDIA PRINTS

The Ever Presents

Sixteen of the many thousands of people who have run the London Marathon over the years have finished every race from the very first in 1981 to the 32nd on the 22 April last year. They are known as the 'Ever Presents'.

This informal group was first acknowledged after the 15th London Marathon in 1995, when it numbered 42. They were awarded with a special commemorative medal, a sweatshirt and guaranteed acceptance in future London Marathons.

The original 42 have now been whittled down to 16. They cover a whole spectrum of running backgrounds, come from all walks of life, different locations and assorted occupations, although many are now retired.

At the top of the list is Chris Finill who received a Guinness World Record certificate in 2010 for "the most consecutive editions of the same World Marathon Majors marathon completed in under three hours".

The following is the full list of ever-present names with their times from the 2012 race and their London PB. More information at www.everpresent.org.uk

Name	Age group	2012 Time	London PB
1 Chris Finill	50-54	2:50:32	2:28:27
2 Michael Peace	60-64	3:34:46	2:38:23
3 Patrick Dobbs	70+	3:48:46	2:31:38
4 Roger Low	65-69	4:07:33	2:33:47
5 Jeffrey Aston	60-64	4:33:48	2:29:34
6 Mike Peel	70+	4:36:00	2:40:30
7 Malcolm Speake	70+	4:44:55	2:45:10
8 Charles Cousens	65-69	4:55:13	2:55:29
9 William O'Connor	65-69	5:04:02	2:34:29
10 David Fereday	70+	5:19:33	2:44:12
11 David Walker	65-69	5:21:59	2:45:48
12 Stephen Wehrle	60-64	5:22:00	2:59:59
13 Terence Macey	60-64	5:38:53	2:58:18
14 Dale Lyons	70+	5:49:03	3:06:48
15 Kenneth Jones	70+	5:50:45	2:55:38
16 Jeffrey Gordon	70+	6:25:33	2:49:54

Twelve made the photo call on the Green Start for the 32nd London Marathon on 22 April 2012: Steve Wehrle, Bill O'Connor, Roger Low, Jeff Aston, David Walker, Charles Cousens, Dale Lyons, Mike Peel, Mike Wilkinson, Pat Dobbs, Mike Peace, Chris Finill

Ever-presents featured in the London Marathon Media Guide 2013. Prepped for another 26.2!

A barber who can cut it in the field

By **LOUISA KENNARD**
louisa.kennard@archant.co.uk

Gearing up to run his 24th marathon

LEN Cousens doesn't have to think about putting his best foot forward when he runs the London Marathon next weekend because he could do it with his eyes shut.

The Beccles barber will be running his 24th marathon, having completed every one since it began in 1981, and is now part of only a 30-strong group who are fondly called the Ever Present club.

Len, who owns Len's Loft in The Walk, is determined to run next year's marathon to make it a quarter century.

But his interest in running began in a peculiar way.

"I didn't start running until I was 36. It all began one Christmas when my wife brought me a tracksuit as a present because she thought I would look good in it."

The 61-year-old is raising money for the seventh time in aid of Great Ormond Street Hospital.

"They are a really good charity and if they can't help children, no one can," he said.

Len has run marathons in New York, Paris and Barbados when he has been holidaying and said his motivation was to take it all in his stride.

His training consists of half marathons around where he lives in Lowestoft and 20-mile runs taking in Burgh Castle and Gorleston.

This year Len has been helped on his way by customer Cliff Cox who has been fundraising in his role of landlord of the Bear and Bells pub. Len is hopeful that together they will raise over £600.

"The customers have been brilliant I haven't even had to ask for sponsorship this year and Cliff's help has been fantastic."

But will he get a medal next year for running for 25 years?

"I don't think anything has been planned, but it would be really nice if they did," he joked.

CHILLING OUT: Len Cousens relaxes after training for the London Marathon. Below, Len at work, cutting a customer's hair. Pictures: LOUISA KE

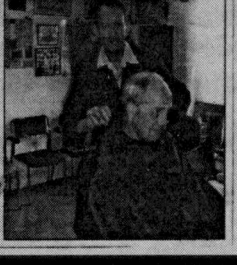

Charles Cousens the Demon Barber, cutting it for Great Ormond Street children in his salon. 2004

The Public Ledger's COMMODITY WEEK

INCORPORATING Daily Freight Register

July 13, 1985

The Public Ledger Cup

1985 London Marathon

THE following Baltic Exchange runners completed the 1985 London Marathon in the times shown against their names. Awarded to the first Baltic runner to finish. The Public Ledger Cup has been retained by E.G. Falck-Therkelsen who also won it in 1984.

E.G. Falck-Therkelsen (Turnbull Scott Chartering)   2hrs. 47mins.

C. Jones (Tatham Bromage & Co.)   2hrs. 51mins.
A.P. Hamilton (International Shipbrokers)   2hrs. 58mins.
D. Grant (John I. Jacobs)   2hrs. 59mins.
D. Wilcox (Stephenson Clarke Shipping)   3hrs. 35mins.
J.P. Watson (J.A. Finzi Laymar Clark & Co.)   4hrs. 52mins.

By completing the 26 miles 385 yards course of the 1985 London Marathon in 2hrs. 47mins., Erik Falck-Therkelsen (right) of Turnbull Scott Chartering won 'The Public Ledger Cup' for the second year in succession. The trophy, awarded to the first participant from a Baltic Exchange member company to complete the tough course, was presented on June 26 by Warwick Hardaker, Publishing Director of The Public Ledger. — see page 9 for a full list of Baltic runners.

Erik Falck-Therkelsen receiving the winners cup after the 1995 London

Running men relax with a marathon after crossing US

Two friends have completed the great American road trip — by foot.

Stephen Pope, 41, far left, and Chris Finill, braved dehydration, traffic and even rattlesnakes running from San Francisco to New York. They did the 31,000-mile trip in 79 days, raising £15,000 for Help for Heroes. "We didn't leave much time to acclimatise," said Mr Pope, from Sheffield. "We got off the plane in San Francisco at 3pm and by 5pm we were running."

The men, who wore out seven pairs of running shoes, finished by taking part in the New York Marathon. "After running 40 miles a day, it seemed like nothing at all," Mr Pope said.

TIMES 22/10/13

Chris Finill celebrate their 3,100 mile TransAm run in 79 days – It's a record!

Thank you card from Gt. Ormond Street Children for Charles Cousens' help.

Runners aiming for 20th finish

South Wales Echo Saturday, April 15th, 2000 — Localnews

By Peter Bibby
peter.bibby@wme.co.uk

FRIENDS Mick McGeogh and Jeff Aston have pounded more of the streets of London than they care to remember.

They were there in the first London Marathon line-up 19 years ago – and enjoyed it so much they kept going back for more.

In fact, Mick, 44, from Barry, and Jeff, 52, from Cardiff, are part of an extra-special running club that boasts just 40 members from all over the world.

They are the only ones who have completed every single London Marathon since the event first started in 1981.

And Mick and Jeff, both members of Cardiff's Les Croupiers Club, will be back again tomorrow for the 20th run.

"The first London Marathon was staged on a soaking wet Sunday in March, but even then we could tell it would grow into the most special race in the world," said Mick, of Cwm Barry Way.

"I shall be nervous before the start as always, but once you're on the road it's such an uplifting experience you just get carried along by the feeling of shared adventure."

Mick's run will help raise money for the Echo-Ty Hafan Children's Hospice Appeal.

But Jeff, a computer systems analyst, of Clos Treoda, Whitchurch, fears he may have to walk the entire 26 miles after damaging a nerve in his back.

"I'm alright if I walk, but once I start running it's very painful," he said.

"But not taking part tomorrow is just not an option. I have to complete the distance to keep up the record, and that will almost certainly mean walking the entire route."

▶ **RECORD BREAKERS** *Jeff Aston, left, and Mick McGeogh are the only people to have completed every London Marathon since 1981.*

PICTURE: Richard Swingler

Mick McGeoch & Jeff Aston the 2000 Welsh Wizard record breakers.

Mike Peel's magnificent moment in 2012 – running the Olympic Torch Relay through Bromley.

Roger Low ripping through London streets in 1991

Dave Clark's Swansong after 30 glorious London's

Dale Lyons aka Galloping Gourmet does the 1st Triple London tossing pancakes in 1998.

Doc Mac Speake really enjoying a sunny 2011 in London - those were the days!

Dave Fereday toughing it out to beat the clock in 2005 against some mean opposition!

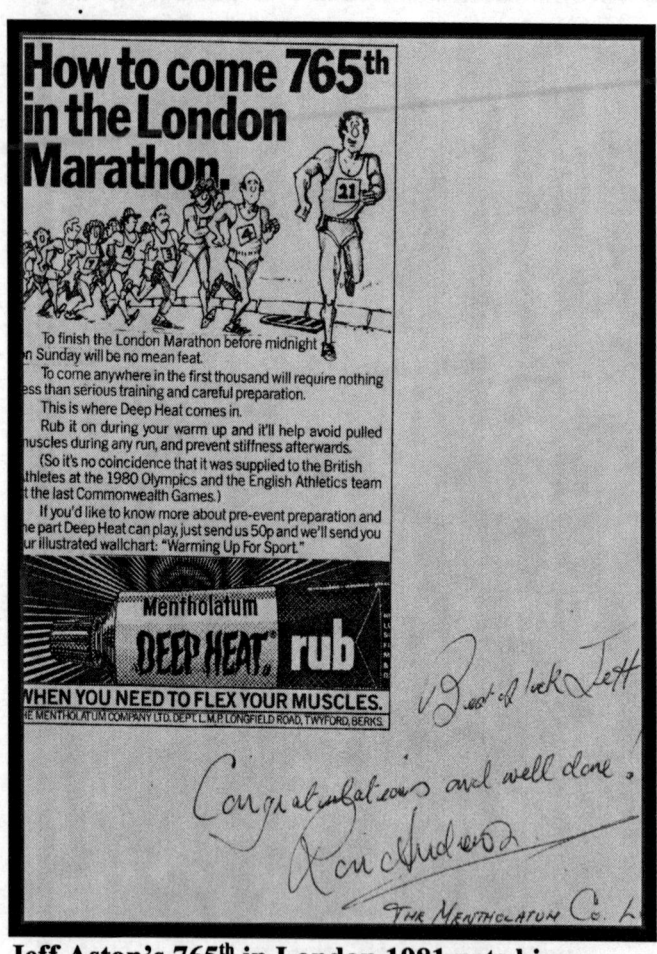

Jeff Aston's 765th in London 1981 nets him a year of vapour rub – he's obviously hot stuff!

**Mike Wilkinson is a Rupert Runner in the
1991   London, with VIP Ron Clarke.**

Orion stalwarts Jeff Messenger- Chris Adams-Bryan Read grasping the Essex O/50 Trophy 1991

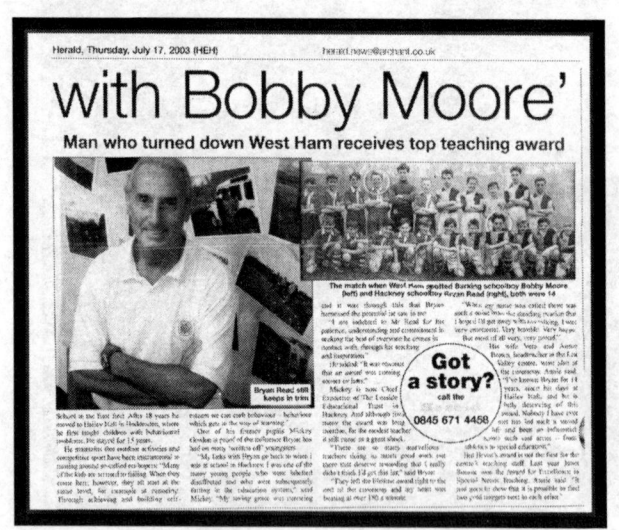

Bryan Read of Hackney Schoolboys played with by Bobby Moore when they were 14.

Orion Club President John Legge enjoying a glass or two at the Presentation Dinner.

The last picture show with eight Everpresents Messrs. L-R Peel, Gordon, Peace, Wehrle, Walker, Low, Aston & O'Conner but where are the other seven?

Chris Finill leads the Olympic London Marathon Trial in 2010 – Ever-present to the fore!

Get a move on Chris or we'll miss the start!

Marathon won't be same without Rainer
72-year-old has done every London race

BY MATTHEW LEGG

THIS year's London Marathon will go ahead without one vital ingredient – marathon man Rainer Burchett.

The 72-year-old will miss the event for the first time in its 32-year history after a knee injury forced him out.

Mr Burchett, of Watermillock, near Penrith, is one of only 18 people to have completed every running of Britain's most famous race.

But his proud record will be broken this year after a knee operation left him unable to walk, let alone run.

The op was required after a gradual deterioration of the knee, which had forced him to walk the course last year – a feat that took more than seven hours.

But despite the setback, he is refusing to retire completely from marathon running and hopes to one day compete again.

"I've known for some time that last year would be my last, but that hasn't made it any easier," he said.

"I'm gutted really and don't know whether I'll even be able to watch on TV this year."

Rainer Burchett: Hoping to run again

Finished: 1996 marathon

Best time: The 1991 marathon

Rainer Burchett bows out of the London after a glorious 32 year run due to failing knees.

Dave Walker with daughter Hannah and son John after a successful 2010 London

CHAPTER 5

International Globetrotters

Ever-presents on Tour.

Introduction
So, let us take a closer and more detailed look at where the EPs running shoes have taken them around the globe. Of the 27 EPs only five have stayed at home. A trawl of each of the five continents, split into their respective countries, cities and runs will pinpoint the amazing places and distances the EPs have travelled in search of their favourite runs.

Heavily favoured by the EPs are the Big City Marathons like New York, Berlin, Paris and Boston while some looked for more iconic, out of the way places or challenging runs such as the Athens and Everest marathons or even the Jungfrau in Switzerland.

Where possible, running times and years will be shown but remember most of these runs were completed many years ago and memories fade. Consider if you will that some EPs have run in excess of 100 marathons with 64 the average over three or more decades of their running careers. A substantial total by any measure.

So where to start this International saga? The most distant, the most popular or the most highly rated? I think we must start with North America and in particular the New York Marathon for a number of reasons. Firstly New York has the allure and magnetism of a great City and secondly the New York is one of the oldest and most highly rated Big City Marathons. Thirdly, it was the inspiration for Chris Brasher's London Marathon initiative and finally the New York provided me with the inspiration for the Real Marathon Men, so what better place to start?

The American Continent

USA;　Canada;　West Indies

New York Marathon

What is so glamorous about the New York Marathon that attracts thousands of British runners like bees to the honey-pot each year? Maybe it is because New Yorkers embrace the marathon and its participants with unparalleled fervour every year. Or, maybe it's the kaleidoscope of spectators cramming the route all the way through the five Boroughs of Staten Island, Brooklyn, Queens, The Bronx and Manhattan. Many restaurants and tourists spots give free rides or generous discounts to marathon runners who are greeted everywhere by New Yorkers like long lost friends.

Or perhaps it's the colourful Parade of Nations from the United Nations Building with the International Breakfast Run up to Central Park the day before the main event. The Marathon finish in Central Park is '*awesome*' with the spectator tumult deafening the runners as they pass the statue of the marathon's creator Fred Lebow (nee Lebowski). Whatever the reason, every runner says it is the one to run.

Naturally, many of the EPs have run New York. Among them Rainer Burchett who has run it four times with a best of 3:09, Terry Macy (4:01), Mike Peace, 1981, (2:52), Steve Wehrle (3:36), Charles Cousens and Erik Falck-Therkelsen.

Roger Low must take the 1st prize for running it twenty times and must know the route like the back of his hand. For running fifteen of them Roger receives an automatic entry every year. Part of the reason for his regularity is that Roger is an American born in Alabama.

Dale Lyons ran it seven times from 1981 (3:11) to 2004 and one of those in 2001 was two months after 9/11 when the City authorities had considered cancelling the race. *"The security before the race was really tight but the atmosphere was incredibly emotional with the fire fighters and police cherry-pickers lining the route"*, said Dale.

In the 1990 event Chris Finill managed to break his big toe and still ran a 2:52 marathon – incredible!

The Saginaw Marathon

Chris does clearly remember quite a bit of his first, the Saginaw Marathon in Michigan in that he hitch-hiked there, slept on a gym floor and then ended up after the race in an ambulance after his time of 2:40. Didn't Simon & Garfunkel hitch-hike from Saginaw too?

After their TransAm run of over 3,000 miles Chris Finill and Steve Pope, both completed the New York marathon in 2011 in an amazing 3:38.

Presumably they still had some energy left! More importantly they raised £15,000 for the charity 'Help for Heroes'!

The Boston Marathon

Boston is only second to Athens as the oldest Marathon and is one you have to qualify for as it tends to attract the better quality runners e.g. EPs, as its numbers are ring fenced! That was until the Centenary in 1996 when an unprecedented 42,000 were entered with 30,000 qualifiers, 10,000 in a ballot and another 2,000 added later to offset any gate-crashers. It was the first of the computer *'chipped'* marathons and coined the warning to runners *'no chip no medal'*.

Just two days before the Marathon the City was blanketed in snow, shutting the airport but the weather gods relented and on the day the sun shone and temperatures rose to enable five EPs to take part. They were Mike Peel (3.30.00), Rainer Burchett, Dale Lyons (3:43), Mike Peace (2:55) and Steve Wehrle (4.30). If their times in the 1996 London were a trifle tardy a wholly acceptable excuse was that the Boston was only six days earlier!

The Detroit Marathon

This is a two country marathon which starts in Windsor, Canada then continues into the USA via the Detroit River tunnel, part of the Great Lakes and finishes in Detroit City. In 1998 Mike Wilkinson finished in a useful 3:56:35 and to ensure clean air for the runners they closed the tunnel the night before; how considerate!

The Rocky Mountain Marathon
Erik Falk-Therkelsen likes to travel, so when he was in Canada's Alberta in 1996 he decided to enter the Rocky Mountain Marathon in Canmore. The undulating course through towering mountains took him a very respectable 3:17 and a 2nd place finish in the O/50's category, a record he is rightly proud of.

Montreal 24 hr Championships
On his travels again Chris Finill proudly represented Britain in the World 24 hour Championships, in September 2007 in Drummondville Canada.

The Chicago Marathon
The big Windy City marathon was the attraction for Mike Peace in 2010 and despite the draughty route he still managed to run a 5:09. Rainer Burchett also ran the same year and finished in the same time as Mike. Was it a race and who won?

The Houston Marathon
Rainer Burchett was the only EP to run the 1980 Houston Marathon in 3:37 and rated the setting and the organisation typical of the US marathons - awesome!

The Miami Marathon
Running for the 1st time in Florida, the Sunshine State, Dave Fereday posted a very respectable 2:50:07 in the 1980's.

The South Carolina Half
Working for a while in the Southern states Roger Mawer ran the Carolina half marathon with some friends in the 1990's, just to keep himself fit

The Barbados Marathon
This must have been a joy to run for Dave Fereday in 1989 for a 3:11:19 and Charles Cousens in 1987, with balmy breezes and an exotic setting on a tropical island. We're green with envy!

The European Continent

Greece, Ireland, France, Italy, Germany, Switzerland, Hungary, Channel Islands, Spain, Lanzarote, Majorca and Holland. Greece

The Athens Marathon
Europe is far and away the most popular continent for EPs with no fewer than thirteen countries in their bag with Paris and Berlin Marathons the favourites.

There is however, no other place in Europe to start than in Greece because Pheidippides started all this rigmarole back in Marathon in 490 BC with a run of 24.85 miles from Marathon to Athens. Without this event there would have been no London Marathon and of course no Real Marathon Men book to write.

But why is it now 26.2 miles? Apparently, the 1.35 miles were added because the favoured course from Windsor to the White City for the 1908 Olympic event was 26 miles. Then an extra 0.2 of a mile (or 385 yards} was added so the finish would be adjacent to the Royal Box of King Edward VII who intended that Queen Alexandra and their children would have ringside seats. It was not until 1924 that 26.2 was officially accepted as the marathon length.

Peter Shepheard, was one of two EPs to take on the Athens Marathon in October 1983, and at the time wished he hadn't! At 8 a.m. when the race was scheduled to begin, the temperature hit a decidedly warm 32c but an anti-government demonstration delayed the start until midday by which time the thermometer was hovering around 40c. Not a time to run any distance let alone 26.2!

To make matters worse Peter was advised not to drink the water as it could be contaminated and it was not until the 32k mark that he managed to drink some coca-cola. Peter takes up the story. *"I struggled to the finish along Constitution Avenue towards Athens with cars blaring their horns with their engines on. It was 100% noise and 100% CO2 pollution"*. Having the resolve of an EP however he finished in the Olympic Stadium in 2:50:54 in 18th place and 2nd O/40. A truly remarkable time in those conditions!

The other EP to last the pace was Mike Wilkinson who ran it in 1997 and finished in the old Olympic

Stadium in 117th place with a time of 3:15:50 just shading the 3rd placed Soviet lady. He was quite overcome when the Russian athlete grabbed him at the finish to give him a BIG kiss!

Ireland

The Dublin Marathon
Twice on the Shamrock Isle, Mike Peace ran Dublin in very fast times of 2:42 and 2:45 in the mid 1980's. He was proud to say he stayed in the same B & B as the winners! But didn't they get HIS autograph?

France

The Paris Marathon
Another splendid 26.2 in the spring is the Paris Marathon, rarely more than a week adrift of the London and a run that has attracted many EPs over the years.

Charles Cousens ran with his wife in 1987; Jan Hildreth enjoyed a lovely day there; Roger Low won a pair of running shoes in 2005 with a sub 3 hour run; Peter Greenwood had a good run in the 1980's and Dave Walker and Jeff Gordon also participated manfully.

This delightful run takes the marathoners through all the well known parts of Paris. Up the Champs Elysee, down Le Place de la Concorde, past the Louvre, around the Arc de Triomphe, just missing the Cathedrale de Notre Dame, through the Tuilleries

Gardens, close to the Sacre Coeur in Montmartre, and over the Pont Neuf. It's like running through a tourist's guide book!

Not far from Paris is the **Taverny Marathon** where in 1982 Dave Fereday ran a 2:54.39 and another sub 3 for the EP *'Metronome man'*.

The Somme Marathon

Through the First World War battlefields near Marley, the Somme Marathon provides a poignant reminder of the enormous cost in human lives between 1914 and 1918. Jeff Gordon was acutely aware of this as he ran along the rural route to finish in another sub 3 hour time.

La Trans Baie run (Bay of the Somme)

One endurance race Ray Johnson recalls was the Trans Bay Race in France, across the Bay of the Somme through mud and water, waist deeps. Ray *'enjoyed'* it so much he returned with his Striders club three times - brave or foolhardy? You decide!

The Marathon du Medoc

If you want to do the most bizarre, off the wall marathon anywhere the Marathon du Medoc in Pauillac, near Bordeaux should be on every serious marathoner's *'to do'* list. Advertised as *'Le Plus Longue Marathon du Monde'* (the longest marathon in the world) it may be, by about 400 yards (according to my Garmin GPS). Everyone is in fancy dress carnival attire that changes each year and everyone, apart from a few dozen serious runners, treats it as a fun run, and why not? There are few rules about how you meander through twenty three, **yes 23**, *'haut chateaux'* vineyards, on scooters, bikes, rickshaws, wheelchairs, sitting on a *'steamroller'* or you can even run it! Some 8,000 do each year, but get your application in early.

Very good quality wine is *'en situe'* at each vineyard, although you're not obliged to sample. And, for those who like to dawdle along hoping to sneak under the relaxed six hour plus cut off time there's always buckets of fresh Arcachon oysters to consume two miles from the finish.

Three EPs have competed this singular marathon. Rainer Burchett, who else, in a leisurely 5:20; Dale Lyons in 2012 who forgot his carbo gels so took an agonising 6:18 in the 35c temps and was rescued by his running friend Colin from the French medics. Peter Greenwood also enjoyed the experience.

The Dordogne Marathon

Down into the beautiful rural centre of France the Dordogne is a tourist paradise. *"Where better to organise a marathon, passing through the lush countryside?"* thought Jeff Gordon. He found out by running it in 2:49 in 1981 and put the icing on the cake by finishing 2nd!

Italy

The Florence Marathon
If you want a taste of history in a city of marble and culture then this was the place that Rainer Burchett chose to combine both in the autumn of 2009 and run a marathon as well.

The out and back course to the centre of Florence is dominated by the Duomo Cathedral then winds its way along the Arno River before crossing the ancient Ponte Vecchio to the finish. Rainer carded a relaxed four hour time for the run.

Germany

The Berlin Marathon
Ten EPs ran this fanatically supported marathon by the locals. Three EPs ran before the wall came down and seven afterwards. Starting in West Berlin Dale Lyons ran in 1987 with a 3:14 *"the crowds were wall to wall and six deep for the whole race";* Terry Macy in 1986 and Charles Cousens in 1987 with a 3:15 and thought he *"ran really well"*. The marathon organiser shipped in mountains of food during and after the race for the runners, including **spaghetti bolognaise** and then closed a whole street to erect mobile showers for the unisex runners and what views the EPs had!

After a very speedy run after the Wall came down in November 9th 1989, Jan Hildreth was selected as a trialist for the Commonwealth Games. Then Jeff Aston ran in 1997 in a quick time of 2:53 and remembers it for his first computer chipped marathon and *"the wall of noise"* all around the course.

The overall organisation was superb. Visits after the marathon to East Berlin were a chastening and daunting experience with uniforms and queues everywhere. Prices were a fraction of the West but food in many of the shops was minimal and restaurant décor more reminiscent of the 1930's.

After the Wall crumbled, the historic Brandenburg Gate fronted the marathon start and with the watch towers gone the mood was effervescent. Peter Greenwood had his fastest marathon with a very quick time of 2:37:18. Ray Johnson ran in 1990 as did Rainer Burchett who posted a 3:02. In 1997, Jeff Aston finished in 2:53 and also remembers the *"wall of noise"*; all around the course. Mick McGeoch ran in 2001, winning the O/45's prize in a fast sub 3 hour time. Steve Wehrle and Mike Peace were also part of the EP contingent.

A great marathon and an enlightening but sobering experience in the EPs opinion..

European 'Ironman' Roth

A tiny village in Bavaria held the 1992 European Ironman which was also a qualifier for the original Ironman in Hawaii. Almost 1,800 international competitors started the swim section in two waves of 850 in a deserted shipping canal and created a mini bow wave at the gun. Three laps covered the 112 mile bike section with the marathon a straight out and back through woods, paths and villages. An idyllic setting for Dale Lyons and his three colleagues from the Coventry Triathlon Club. Dale's finishing times of 4:22 for the marathon and 11:35 overall earned him 1st O/50 UK entrant but well off the pace for a Hawaii place. *"The international opposition was too hot"*, he said regretfully.

Switzerland

The Jung Frau Marathon

One of the tougher mountain marathons in Switzerland is the Jung Frau Marathon that rises to the giddy 6,857ft Kleine Scheidegg which is *"often snow covered despite being an Autumn event,"* according to Ray Johnson. He confirmed that *"it was very hard, very cold and very wet"* so there must be something of the masochist in his make-up but he did battle to finish in a gruelling 6:09 in 1994; well done Ray!

The Swiss Mountain Marathon

Probably the toughest summer ultra marathon has a start in Davos, climbs to over 8,000 ft, and stretches for 43 miles! In 1995 Dale Lyons completed it in 10:57:20, and just to add to his difficulties he tossed a pancake all the way accompanied by the mega marathon runner Dave Phillips of Massey Ferguson RC. They're obviously not all locked up yet! Dale remembered that *"One female runner from the USA got a real shock when she realised it was 43 miles and not 43km, the marathon length,"* and only eighteen miles further!

Hungary

The Budapest Marathon
To the strains of the Strauss waltz the Budapest Marathon follows the winding Blue Danube for the 4,000 runners, unperturbed by only a sprinkling of spectators. Not put out by this apparent lack of interest Terry Macy managed to post a quick 3:17 in 2001 and considered it a *"good one to do!"*

Channel Islands

Isles of Scilly Marathon
The Scilly Isles are not very big, so how many circuits are there to complete a marathon Dave Fereday wondered? After winning he found out; six times! Having completed the run three times in 1982, 1983, and 1986 his times were all within an amazing two minutes of each other. He declined to reveal how many finished although 46 started!

Spain

The Benidorm Marathon
Our sole representative for the 2nd time in the 1984 'Costa del Sol was Dave Fereday. In a time to keep the locals at bay with a 2:52:25 and fast enough for his 2nd O/40 place, he was just pipped at the finish by *'running man'* and British icon Ron Hill.

Lanzarote

The La Santa Challenge week on the windy, volcanic Canary island is a favourite with many club runners requiring a spring tune-up before the running season or the London Marathon. A raft of runs from 10k to 25k and a 7 mile trail run comprises the challenge so Steve Wehrle, a big fan and participant, took it up and did them all; a great *'feet'* obviously!

Majorca

Velde Marathon

In another of the sub tropical isles Mick McGeoch did another superb time in the Velde Marathon in 2007 with a 2:52:00 to claim the 2nd prize in the O/50 category.

Holland

The Rotterdam Marathon

The only EP on record to run marathons in Holland was Mike Wilkinson in the 1987 Rotterdam Marathon which is considered to be one of the fastest marathon courses having attracted a number of world marathon records over the years. Mike didn't quite break any records, finishing in comfortable 3:18:41

He then ran the Westland Marathon on the Hook of Holland in 1990 in 3:00:43 just missing out on a sub 3 hour. Mike was given first aid for severe calf cramps and narrowly escaped a CPR (heart booster) team when he fell asleep on the recovery stretcher. His

Amsterdam Marathon was notable because he cannot remember when it was or in what time he finished!

The African Continent

South Africa

The Comrades Marathon
From South Africa's Pietermaritzburg to Durban, the Comrades Marathon is not content with a single 26.2 but a whopping 56 mile ultra trek with a bite. Run through arid plains and searing temperatures the Comrades is run *'up'* one year from Durban and *'down'* the next from Pietermaritzburg on alternate years. This ultra attracts the world's top marathoners, among whom was Alberto Salazar, who broke the world marathon record in New York in 1981. Now in his dotage he is Mo Farah's trainer and guru.

In 2003 Chris Finilll also took up the ultra baton to finish a *'down'* in 6:41, and it's not all downhill! This is top order ultra running in any category but remember Chris was fifty seven at the time!

Rainer Burchett took on the Comrades twice starting at 6 a.m. on both occasions, the first in 1997 with a *'down'* run in 8:42, winning a bronze medal and then with an *'up'* eleven years later in 11:01. Rainer stated that he was *"seriously exhausted"* after the run and who wouldn't be after 56 miles and 68 years of age?

Two Oceans Marathon

The Two Oceans Marathon, is a 35 miles jaunt along an incredibly beautiful North Cape route near Cape Town that Mike Peace enjoyed running in the 1980's.

The Asian Continent

Russia

The Moscow Marathon

Under and around the minarets of Moscow in the middle of a roasting summer in 1987, Terry Macy ran a marvellous time of 3:01 in the conditions. *"Some of the Russians were running the race in bare feet and afterwards were pestering the Westerners for any old trainers."* said Terry. Sign of the times!

India

The Poona Marathon

On the Indian sub continent near Mumbai in 1991 Mick McGeoch ran a superb marathon to post a fast time of 2:39:11, but narrowly missed out on the prizes.

Nepal

The Everest Marathon
Rainer Burchett was asked if he had visited Nepal. *"Yes"* he replied. *"Did you go to Everest?"* was the enquiry *"No"*, .Rainer said, *"I went to have a run!"* Ha! Ha! Of course, he finished the grindingly difficult Everest Marathon.

This was part of the 1997 Diane Penny Sherpani tour to the top of the world for one of the toughest challenges going. After struggling with altitude sickness he still finished with his head up in 9:16.

The Bhutan Marathon
The Everest did not put Rainer off high altitude runs because ten years later he completed the Bhutan Marathon with a trip lead by Mike Gratton, a London Marathon winner in the 1980's.

You need a very good head for heights for this Marathon as the route climbs to the Che La Pass at 12,000 ft. requiring the runners to acclimatise during the trek to the start. Despite taking about four hours longer than expected and finishing in the dark, Rainer was still ahead of many Nepalese and British runners to take the first O/50 prize. A toughness rating for this run would be off the scale with only 16 out of 41 finishers, a drop out of around 60%!

Taiwan

Taipei

The Peoples Republic of China hosted the World's 100 k Championships in 2003 and naturally representing Great Britain was Chris Finill. He rocketed over the mountainous course of 63 miles in 8:03 with a marvellous 16th place out of 200 in a world class field.

The Australasian Continent

New Zealand

The Hamilton Marathon

This is about as far as you can go around the World to run a marathon before turning back home. Near to the famous New Zealand hot-springs of Rotarua is a marathon with all the home comforts. So, when Mike Wilkinson finished the race in 1992 in a quickish time of 3:15 he spent the rest of the day soaking his exhausted body in the bath's warm mineral waters with, he said *"very pleasant company"*.

The Wellington Half

In the South of the North Island whilst on holiday, Roger Mawer was encouraged to run the Wellington Half in the 1990's. He can't remember his time but he does recall beating the NZ ladies All Blacks Rugby team's Captain by some distance.   Well, it's good to beat the All Blacks at anything!

Chapter 5 Summary

On this evidence, 21 of the 26 EPs who have travelled the globe have done their bit in flying the Union Jack for Britain. Across five continents; in dozens of countries; covering hundreds of marathons, exactly how many is difficult to say; across many time zones to the far reaches of what used to be the Empire, the EPs have searched for the Shangri La of marathons. Question! Is there a Shangri La Marathon and if not, what an opportunity?

In fact, the EPs have left almost no country unvisited in their search for the best (New York), the smallest (Bhutan), the biggest (Boston), the most exotic (Barbados), the highest (Everest) and the toughest (Comrades) marathons and ultras (TransAm) around the world in building their impressive running CV's.

But which of the EPs has run the most international marathons and who is the fastest? Well, Roger Low has 20 New Yorks to his credit. But what about Mick McGeoch with his six Berlins and a raft of others in Europe and the Far East? Then there is Dave Fereday with his clutch of American, European and Scilly Isles runs. Has Rainer Burchett perhaps pipped them all with his amazing collection of US and Euro runs coupled with the *'full house'* of the Comrades ultras? Or is it Dale Lyons with his seven New Yorks, European runs, his TransAm relay, (that is 8 marathons worth) and his Euro Ironman?

No! It must be agreed there is only one contender and that is Chris Finill. With his 5 continent runs, his bag of marathons and 100k races, the double Comrades ultras and the most stupendous of all, his TransAm with Steve Pope. All others pale into relative insignificance by comparison to Chris's achievements on the world's stage. Surely, he is without doubt the uber athlete across the range.

This then has been a who's who or what's what of international running experiences, enveloped in an amazing kaleidoscope of mixed cultures and extremes of distant running that must have tested the EPs to the limit. They came through with something to spare it has to be said.

Their missions were not just based on personal interest but often in the altruistic pursuits of helping others. Witness the sums raised for Help for Heroes and the Macmillan Nurses by Chris Finill's and Dale Lyons' relay team on their trans American jaunts. Many other EPs have raised tens of thousands for charities large and small by their globe-trotting performances.

Without question this chapter has covered the crème de la crème of the globe's long distant runs, and runners. The EPs of course!

CHAPTER 6

Riveting Records around the World

What is a record? Information to store for later reference perhaps? An individual statistic that counts as a marker or implies a status? A particular performance that is worthy of group recognition? The creating or breaking of a new or previous performance standard?

In terms of the EPs it embraces all of these definitions. Records for one reason or another provide a means of creating or achieving a higher standard of performance in some sport or activity. Long distance running in the EPs case!

Every EP has a record of some intrinsic significance that stands as a marker for their feelings of accomplishment whether on a personal, club, national or even international level. If they achieve nothing else, a PB (personal best) is a '*record*' that most runners value in their running lifetime.

Which EPs then, if any, has the '*best record*'? At the end of the chapter we will be better able to decide, or perhaps not.

Take, for example, Dave Fereday's '*fetish*' in keeping a defining performance log of all his races over the years, which he says provides the necessary base for his improvements. It also makes for engrossing reading, and not just for Dave.

Or, look at the 23 Log Books of Dale Lyons, initially developed from the **Adidas * Jog Log** initiative. These contain the details of every training run and race since 1979, the year he started running as a serious pastime and provides a comparative and motivational base for his training and races.

* **Adidas Jog Log.** Adidas initiated the Jog Log in the early 1980's by providing free jogging record books which were linked to badges for hours jogged, up to the Super-jogger badge for 240 recorded hours.

Record comparisons
Is one record better than another? The decision will often depend on who you ask or what the record is compared to. Yes, you could argue that a Gold Medal is better than a Silver or a Silver having more kudos than a Bronze. But a Silver for someone expecting a Gold could be less attractive than a Bronze for someone who had expected neither. Witness the ecstatic celebrations of Tom Daley's Bronze in the 10 metre Olympic final in the 2012 Games against the muted celebrations of the Chinese diver who won Silver when he fully expected Gold. All records in that respect are relative.

Record satisfactions
What record provides the most pleasure or the most gratification? The fastest? The longest? The toughest? The highest? Again, it would to a degree depend on one's expectation for the event. Rainer

Burchett's Everest Marathon finish time in over 9 hours would not be counted as his most enjoyable given the circumstances. It was certainly his highest, and he may say it was his greatest achievement, given its toughness rating. At the other end of the scale Rainer's 10k best time of 37:30 might have given him the same surge of achievement at the time.

A high toughness rating would certainly be accorded to Dale Lyons' triple London in 1998, having to run through the night, nursing a broken wrist for the 17:12 slog at the youthful age of 61 years *"I wasn't tired after the first two so thought I'll do one more"* he joked *"but more importantly I had my charity sponsorship tripled!"*

The Isles of Scilly Marathon is obviously a well guarded secret because Dave Fereday, at 44 was the oldest in the race - amazing! In addition he must have been surprised and delighted when mounting the winners podium after a time of 2:52:03 to be presented with the winners trophy by non-other than Prime Minister Harold Wilson.

We can all be flabbergasted at Chris Finill's achievement at having run for five decades of marathons in sub 3 times, his TransAm record and his continuous sub 3 hour Londons. These are sublime records without doubt, but to an athlete who runs a sub 3 hour marathon by one second in 2:59:59 is to them, no less an achievement. This particular 'high' was hard earned by a certain Steve Wehrle in the 1991 London and is his crowning London '*record*'.

One of Max Jones's many glittering successes in his illustrious running career would have been retaining the Founders Trophy in the Comrades Marathon in 1999, but was the first time even better?

Achievement and pleasure are two of the defining reasons for running any distance. And these were Peter Shepheard's feelings at the finish of the Shaftesbury 10 mile race because he had just beaten Dave Bedford, by two minutes! His actual time was an irrelevance.

'Enjoyable' Runs

Although Roger Low has run 20 New York City marathons he says his most enjoyable marathon is *"any one, when I've finished"*! We would all empathise with that sentiment. Roger might never have had a more satisfying feeling when he was given automatic entry to the New York after running the iconic marathon 15 times. Almost a New York Ever-present perhaps?

New York marathon times rarely come up to expectations however, because there is so much to see and so much to do and so many places to visit in Manhattan. Mike Peace, one of our faster sub 3 hour runners, would have been highly delighted with his 2:52 in 1981 after all the sightseeing and excitement of his first Trans-Atlantic marathon. On the other hand he may, at the time have been just as delighted when, as part of the Ranelagh Harriers 3 man relay team, he broke the record for the South Downs Way

Most Marathons

Top spot in this category has to go to Pete Greenwood with 176. narrowly edging out Mike Wilkinson's *'over'* 150 total. Next on the *'madness'* scale is 'Doc' Mac Speake with 120 closely followed by Jeff Gordon with 'over 100'. Roger Low is also in the '100' club. Another centurion is Max Jones who achieved his Holy Grail of marathons in the 1999 London in an amazing time for a 71 year old of 3:42:58.

Just outside the century is Dale Lyons with 92 and with fewest is Alastair Aitken with 21, just two more than his EP run of 19. On the other hand Alistair has lots of fast shorter run times to his credit. So who are the fast guys when you look at shorter distances on track and trail?

Fastest Times

If you are talking records, as in fastest times, then Mick McGeoch's CV is littered with them. At the really fast end of the running spectrum is where Mick won the 1997 British Masters 5,000 in a blistering 15:26 ending with a 64 second last lap. At the other end of the distance scale he has run marathons over forty times at sub 2:30 marathon pace. Most EPs would die for something well over 2:30! Using the experimental *'bleed out' diet,** Mike set his PB (personal best) at 2:17:58 in the 1983 London.

*   **the 'bleed out'** *diet involves starving the body of carbohydrates for two weeks prior to the marathon then a few days before, loading the body with high levels of carbohydrates. The effect of this 'starve - load' reaction apparently shocks the body to take on more than normal levels of carbohydrates, thus extending the body's glycomic reservoir and giving extended life to the muscles at the critical stage of the marathon i.e.around 20 miles..*

When you are talking 'fast for age' records then the 1943 mile race of Max Jones has to be included with the best. Without ANY training he posted an amazing 5:03 when he was a cherubic 16 year old! Only three years later in a varsity 7½ mile cross country match, Max, running for Oxford, came first, shading our first sub 4 minute miler, **Roger Bannister** - what a scalp!

It is a good thing that Bill O'Connor decided to decamp from the antipodes to England in the 1970's otherwise he would never have become an EP. We would then have been deprived of his amazing personal records and ultra fast times for a swathe of distances. These times, set in the 1980's, place him near the zenith of running elite. For example, how many can run a mile in 4:17, 5 miles in 24:40, 10 miles in 51:29, a half marathon in 1:10 or a 20 mile race in 1:53? Thanks for Bill's ability should be credited in part to his English father, a Dunkirk veteran, and his New Zealand mother for their running genes!

At the other end of the speed scale Reg Burbidge may not be the quickest of the EPs but he has one record no-one else will beat. Before the 1995 start Reg was the oldest EP at the grand age of 80. His prediction of *'around 6 hours'* was not too far off the mark with a 6:53:27

Our only US born runner Roger Low has an impressive record in both the New York City Marathon and in vets races in the UK with the following times.

Best place NYC--1982 #340th overall

Best age place NYC--1999 #15th M55

XIII World Vets Athletic Championships, Gateshead--Aug 1999 #24th overall

SCVAC Championships, Abingdon Marathon--2006 First M60-69

BMAF 2009--First Vet 65+

Club Records

Mick McGeoch's marathon total of 73 might be considered modest when compared to some of the other EPs but quality rather than quantity was always Mick's over-riding priority in setting club records. As an example of Mike's quality, he completed a stunning Benidorm Marathon in 1986 in a sizzling time of 2:24 to claim 3rd place.

At club level many of the EPs have set records to place them above the pack, witness Dave Clark's performances across the board. His age related times listed below, for 10k right through a mix of distances to the London to Brighton ultra are something special.

Fastest times: 10k time 33.39 at Grove 10k Oxford 1984;
10 mile age group 45 – 50's – 57:00 Trowbridge 1983;
Half Marathon age group 55 – 60's category – 82:52 in Vets Half 1988:
Marathon age group 45 – 50's – 2:41:56 London;
London to Brighton 7:14:44   1981.

Jeff Aston is also up there with the best with a mile in 4:57 in 1984; a ten mile in 52:51 in 1983 and a half marathon of 1:10:56. His 5k, 10k and 20 mile times are no less impressive in winning him a clutch of club records. His only *'ultra'* was in the 1981 Cardiff Marathon which he said, smiling *"was half a mile over distance."*

Mike Peel's PB (personal best) records for his shorter runs are also rather quick with 53 seconds for 400 metres and 55:30 for 10 miles.

Chelmsford AC was the venue for Jeff Gordon to become the 100 yards club champion when a burgeoning teenager and later on to build on his early promise.

Lining Roger Mawer's *'trophy room'* walls are over 300 running medals and many of these are Club Trophies from his time with the Lowestoft RC. *"They continue to provide a very warm feeling of satisfaction"*, Roger said with some emotion.

Ultra Records

Ultra marathons are usually described as any distance over 27 miles according to the 100 Marathon club. EPs have run many ultras such as the Swiss Mountain Marathon (43 miles) London to Brighton run (53 miles) or the Comrades Marathon.(56 miles).

Even longer ultras are from 100k (63 miles) to 24 hour races and beyond. Mike Wilkinson could be described as the ultra *'hound'* in running four 24 hour races for England in International events. The furthest of his four ultras was in Chorley, Lancashire where he chalked up a PB (personal best) of 117 miles in 24 hours.

In these races athletes can rack up over 150 miles which is usually performed on a track or short circular course. For example, the world record-holder in 2012 for a 24 race was Mike Morton who ran 172.45 miles, that is almost seven marathons worth!

One of the most amazing runs of all was crossing the USA by Chris Finill and his friend Steve Pope in a charity based run in the autumn of 2011. For a continuous total of 79 days and 22 hours (we won't worry about the minutes) they ran across the USA from San Francisco to New York, 3,126 miles, non-stop! In the final week leading to New York they completed 295 miles, maintaining a phenomenal daily average of almost fifty miles!

Chris said the toughest section of the run was during the early stages. Suffering from stress fractures to his tibia when crossing Utah, he ran in padded socks and kept going. Aged fifty two, Chris was giving his younger running partner Steve almost seven years and was one of the oldest to complete the Trans-Am crossing. Phew!

Another trans American run from Washington's White House to San Francisco's Golden Gate Bridge was run by twelve relay runners from Birmingham in August 1995 sponsoring the Macmillan Nurses' charity, for whom they raised the sum of £20,000. As one of the relay team Dale Lyons ran 230 miles for his stint tossing pancakes all the way for a Guinness Book entry which never materialised. Dale recalls an amusing episode. *"Crossing the desert in Utah, miles from anywhere I got some astounded looks from truck drivers, but it was worth it."*

One of the most exhausting runs in the World was the 100k championships, which took place in Tainan County, Taiwan in November 2003. Despite the three limiting '*H*' factors of heat, humidity and hills, Chris Finill, representing Great Britain, came through with flying colours in 14th spot out of an International field of 200 in a time of 8:03. His amazing accomplishments also include representing England and Great Britain fourteen times at 100k and 24 hour runs and winning gold medals at both distances no less!

Another EP record holder in many categories was Max Jones who ran in a 100k race in 1993 to win the O/60 UK title. This was in addition to the Commonwealth O/65 record in the fast time of 9:12:56, almost 7 mph for 63 miles!

In 2013, Mike Peel along with 3 friends tackled the South Downs Way, walking it in a time of 21:51

and with a combined age of 264; was it a Seniors record Mike?

Mac Speake also completed the South Downs Way and finished a little quicker in 13:15. He enjoyed it so much he completed the 100k run twice! Only twice Mac? Erik Falck-Therkelsen has the record for South Downs of TEN circuits and the fastest time of 11:26 for this 80 mile National Trail course. Erik is a club runner of some distinction. The South Downs run is only one of the many ultra events completed by Erik. In 1993 he even bagged the 50-55 age record in a time of 13:36.

Another speedy runner who graduated from early track success to marathons and then into ultras, completing the tough Woodford 40 mile (Essex) in 5 hours was Jeff Gordon. Then, an even tougher test of his stamina and resolve was to survive the Lincoln to Gratham 100k in just over 10 hours in 1981.

The Quasi Ultras

Of course, some marathons become ultras because of their terrain and the variability in their measurement long before GPS technology improved course accuracy. The cross country marathons that easily slide into ultra territory are the Chactonbury Marathon near the South Downs. This is a good 30 miler even if you don't get lost! The Belvoir Challenge (pronounced Beaver) across boggy farmland with checkpoints and feeding stations in Northamptonshire is another for walkers and runners, and a good six hour romp. Dale Lyons the 'Galloping

Gourmet' completed these two in 1990 and 2003 respectively in 3:55 and 6:23 and did he get lost? Yes, both times!

Another cross country marathon/ultra is the Seven Sisters to Beachy Head, undulating its way near the South Downs that Charles Cousens managed to finish *"bushed but not bowed"* in 4:59:22.

Distance is not the only measure for what makes an ultra '*special*' because many are organised to provide the ultimate challenge with the Everest, Bhutan, Jungfrau and the Swiss Mountain marathons as cases in point.

Only one runner has completed a triple London over a 24 hour period. In 1998 Dale Lyons ran the triple starting from Blackheath on the Saturday April 26th at 22.00 hrs. He ran to the Mall arriving at 03.30 a.m. then returned to Blackheath at 8.50 a.m. for the official marathon at 09.30. His times for each run were 5:14; 5:23 and 6:35 and a total of 17:12, running with his arm in a sling due a previous snowboarding accident two weeks earlier!

You could also include triathlons and especially the Ironman version which originated in Hawaii by combining three of that country's toughest sporting challenges. EPs over the years have embraced these challenges with some degree of success and come out on top.

Guinness Records

A few years ago the Guinness Book of World Records decided to get involved with special categories for the London Marathon. Categories such as 'The Tallest Structure' and the 'Fastest Cartoon Character' and the 'Fastest Baby' and even 'The Fastest Female Vegetable' (I'm not joking because I actually met this lady before the 2010 start masquerading as a carrot!). Of course this all adds to the colour, fun and attractiveness of the event. Even the London Marathon itself is a Guinness World Record breaker as the largest annual fund-raising event, raising £52.8 million by 2012.

Die-hard marathoners however, might have a different view and say the London has become more of a fun run or a circus than a proper marathon. Whatever the view, there is no doubt that increased sponsorship for the Marathon have benefited hundreds of charities by these developments.

But to what extent have the EPs become involved in these records? In 1982 Dale Lyons, a former chef tossed a pancake all the way for a new Guinness entry record of 3:09 subsequently improving it in 1996 to 3:06 Not content with one record he went on to break the World Record for the Fastest Egg & Spoon run in the 1990 London, in a time of 3:47 with a certain Chris Brasher signing the egg (guinea fowl). The record was still unbeaten in 2013. He then capped it all in 1995 by setting another new Guinness record for the fastest 3-Legged Marathon in a time of 3:58:28 with his running partner Dave Pettifer of Kenilworth RC.

Another illustrious and fully deserved Guinness Book record was awarded to Chris Finill in 2012 for completing all his London Marathons in less than 3 hours, an amazing sequence. Check the Guinness Book website. Chris said *"I had the flu but was determined to get under 3 hours"* He made it in 2:58:35 – close, and a big cigar for Chris!

Chapter 6 Summary

This chapter has looked at records from a number of perspectives, types and distances in an attempt to put the question of *'records'* into some comparative context.

As seen from the previous chapter on Globe-trotting, records have been set both in the UK and around the world with many in extremes of temperature, distance and height in order to test the most resilient and determined of competitors. The EPs have relished these challenges without question.

At the beginning of the chapter the question was asked who has the best record. Well, the EPs over the past thirty three years have done more than set personal, club, national, international and Guinness World records. Many of these at elite levels and others you would find difficulty believing if the evidence was not set in stone.

So whether you consider speed, endurance, distance or incredulity the criteria for judging the *'best'* record, take your pick, there are plenty to chose from. If you were to ask the remaining 39 EPs this question, you would probably get 39 different answers, at least!

CHAPTER 7

Media links to the Marathon Men

Introduction

Once a year, around March, there is an explosion of interest in the London Marathon and EPs in particular. Local and national papers, radio stations and magazines all want to jump on the collective bandwagon of interest in the highly promoted and televised soap opera that is the London Marathon phenomenon.

Some EPs are contacted between the Londons as happened recently with a call from London Marathon's Head of Publicity Nicola Okey who wanted an EP for an Athletics Weekly interview. Others will be chased after the Marathon for follow ups and to discover what charity sponsorship they have generated. Athletics journals are usually very supportive of runners' requests as it is often a case of mutual interest at work.

This mutual interest was given a boost recently when a plea to Athletics Weekly resulted in an additional number of EPs contributing to the book.

Human interest

Interest in the active EPs sometimes take the form of, *'will they stay EPs after this marathon'* or *'will Chris Finill maintain his sub 3 hour record?'* In the Marathon Handbook of 2005 Reg Burbidge was interviewed as the oldest EP at 80 to question if he would actually finish – he did and under 7 hours. Five other EPS were featured in the same article; Mike Peel, Mike Peace, Ray Johnson, Dale Lyons and Chris Finill whose aim *"was to make his 50th journey round the course, in 2031 – age 72!"* Neasa MacErlean's article *'The Joys of Life on the Run'* stated that each EP had run 660 miles in their 25 Londons to date (actually 655). This total has, in 2013, risen to 865 miles and counting!

On the BBC's website for the same year Dave Clark and Steve Wehrle were lauded as EPs after the 2005 marathon and quizzed on their memories of the first London. Steve wondered if he could actually complete the distance and Dave didn't realise what an impact that first one was going to make.

David Cuffley's article (April 21st 1994) in the Eastern Evening News on Mike Wilkinson's astonishing recovery from a serious knee injury to run the 1994 London in 3:50, his fourteenth, provided a clear insight into the resolve of this particular EP.

Radio; local, national & Internet

Jeff Aston recalls being interviewed on Radio Wales and heralded as *'The only man in Wales to run every London Marathon'*.

A BBC Radio WM (West Midlands) presenter Ed Doolan was amazed to discover in a 2010 interview that Dale Lyons 'The Galloping Gourmet' had run one London, tossing pancakes all the way. Harry Carpenter, the long serving BBC TV presenter of

Sportsnight ate one of Dale's pancakes for a £50 charity contribution, little realising that the spare pancake had lain undisturbed in his shorts for the entire marathon.

As part of the BBC's outside broadcasting team before the 2002 London, Alastair Aitken was asked by BBC's Clare Lidington to comment on the marathon and also discuss his new book *'Athletics Enigmas'*.

Clare Balding of BBC Radio 5 live interviewed Dale Lyons on Blackheath before the 1998 London immediately before Dale's 3rd of the day. Jasper Carrot had loaned him his hotel room for a quick shower and brush up.

Newspapers

In a very long piece in the Times Race Preview before the 1997 London, Mick McGeoch was congratulated for being *'more reliable and faster than London Transport buses'*. Never faster than 2:17 and never slower than 2:31. Mentioned in the same article was the letter Mick wrote to Guinness Book's Norris McWhirter in 1970 when he was 14 year old, saying he thought he could beat the long distance running record of 120 miles at the time. Norris replied that he was too young but to keep training. Fortunately Mick took his advice on board!

Nigel Dempster's Marathon Diary in the March 30th 1981 edition of the Daily Mail is quoted as saying. *"Thanks to the company of Jan Hildreth, 49, the former Director--General of the Institute of Directors and a leading light of Thames Hare and Hounds, the world's oldest cross-country club, the first five miles passed enjoyably but slowly."*

The Birmingham Mail of March 7th 1983 featured three London runners, two from the GPO, Tom McCook ex President of Birchfield Harriers, Peter Green a Mails Efficiency manager and Dale Lyons Head of the Birmingham College of Food, tossing a pancake! They were all sponsoring the Muscular Dystrophy Charity in London's third marathon and Dale was hoping to break his 3:09 pancake record.

Our only hairdressing EP was featured in an article by Louisa Kennard for his local newspaper in March 2004, just before the 24th London. Charles Cousens, 61 was pictured clipping away in his salon *'Lens Loft'* in Lowestoft and said *"I didn't start running until I was 36 when my wife bought me a track suit"* That's right, blame the wife! The rest as they say, is history with Charles still in the running and clipping after his 33rd London.

A local Norwich newspaper reported in June 1984 that Mike Wilkinson would *"never again"* do the 80 mile South Downs Way. *"It wasn't the distance it was the terrain, all chalk and flints"*, Mike said ruefully, although he did finish 30th out of 334 in a fast 15:19:32 and was *'quite pleased with his time.'*

Mike Peel and Alan Pickering, a blind runner were featured in the Bromley Times of May 17th 1984 when Mike escorted Alan to a London Marathon finish of 4:11 which the paper called *'Miraculous for a blind man'*.

The most recent article on the EPs was in the 22nd October 2013 issue of The Times, covering the TransAm crossing of Chris Finill and Steve Pope. The piece pictured the Union Jack waving duo after their historic '31,000' (sic) mile trek (should have been 3,100 ed!). The article was only 2 years late as their run finished with the New York Marathon in October 2011! California to Coney Island, and then the NY marathon on day 80, their rest day! See a record of Chris and Steve's exploits on youtube.
http://www.youtube.com/watch?v=zBYlNXDur-s

Jeff Aston and Mick McGeoch were featured in the South Wales Echo on Saturday April 10th 2000 and talked about their preparation for that year's London Marathon, their 20th. Jeff feared he might have to walk due to a back problem but said *"not taking part is not an option, I have to complete the distance to keep up the record"* and Mick said he was nervous about the Marathon *"but once you're on the road it's such an uplifting experience, you just get carried along by the feeling of a shared adventure."*

David Powell's Times article on reviews of sporting books wrote this about Alastair Aitken's book *"The Winning Edge"*. *'It covers immense ground. Based on interviews with athletes over more than 30 years, Aitken reveals a broad range of experiences and analyses what drives them towards success, whether at the Olympics or on a veterans' cross-country."*

Norwich Evening News reported on April 15th 2005 that despite leg blood clots, Mike Wilkinson was determined to run his 25th consecutive London and maintain his EP status. Brave or foolhardy?

A 25th London Marathon centre-piece by Tom Price in the April 16th 2005 edition of the Daily Express featured Dale Lyons running in a Great Bustard costume for his charity. He said *"The best thing about the London is that it is as much a festival as a race. There's a lot of audience involvement."*

Newbury AC's star runner Dave Clark had to call time on his London Marathon EP status after 30 years, as reported in his local newspaper the Newbury Weekly News on April 29th 2010. Although he finished the marathon in 5:18:49, his fall at 20 miles left him battered and bruised. Dave said *"I could carry on but if I did next year I would have to do it for the next five and then I would be 79"* It wasn't all doom and gloom for Dave because he was presented with his club's Marathon Shield as recognition for his club record of 30 consecutive Londons.

Our ultra marathoner Mike Wilkinson was featured twice in the Eastern Evening News for his 107 mile stroll in the 1989 Milton Keynes 24 hour race and for another 104 mile walk/run in Blackpool 1990 as part of the Europa Cup competition. Mike came 12th despite shin splints and then with Roger Gibbons they grabbed the 3rd team prize from a strong Russian team for their combined distance of 216 miles.

Television

After 3,000 miles running in relays from Washington to San Francisco, 12 runners were videoed by the local Frisco TV channel running across the Golden Gate Bridge to complete their TransAm 12 day marathon in September 1995 One of the team, the pancake tossing ex.chef Dale Lyons said *"it was a spectacular day , no fog and clear views across the Bay to Alcatraz Island."*

In June of 2012 the BBC TV outside camera team were fizzing all over the British Isles to film the Olympic Torch Relay running EPs. The four EPs were Bill O'Connor, running around the streets of Haringey near Alexandra Palace, the original centre for the BBC; Mike Peel in Bromley, Kent; Jeff Gordon through the streets of Wandsworth, South London and Ken Jones in Strabane, Northern Ireland. Without doubt, it was the high point of their year and another mark of national recognition for the EPs.

Before the start of the 2009 London Marathon a group of EPs were quizzed by Jonathan Edwards for the BBC TV Outside Broadcasting Unit on their role and expectations for the run.

An hour BBC TV documentary entitled 'London Marathon Heroes' was broadcast before the 2005 London Marathon and featured a number of EPs including *'The Galloping Gourmet'* making pancakes in his Rugby kitchen.   See **appendix 7 Letter 2005 BBCTV 'Heroes'**

German TV dropped in on the 2013 marathon and spent some time recording the EPs in various states of undress where they were posing for the annual EPs group photo at the Green Start. When asked how they knew about us, they said we were famous in Germany. We told them we were quite famous here too.

Published Books

In his book The London Marathon, John Bryant gives fulsome praise to a number of EPs for their amazing running sequence over the years in the London Marathon.

The 'Athletics Enigmas' was a sports book written by our own EP Alastair Aitken and reviewed by The Book Guild. It covered the lives of some of running's elite, including Gordon Pirie and Haile Gebrselassie. Interviews of these running icons were conducted by Alastair himself for his book. Commenting on the book, Geoff Harrold a former Marathon and Distance Runner editor said *"One of Alastair's best points is that he always asks good questions."* Alastair is also the author of two more books, *The Winning Edge* and *More than Winning* and has been a regular contributor of articles in Athletics Weekly.

Dale Lyons' Autobiography *'33 Sycamore' 'A search for recognition'* published in 2012 had a chapter entitled *'Marathon Mania'* which covered many years of marathons and featured some of the EPs.

Journals

Athletics Weekly is a very popular publication for runners and Alastair Aitken, was a regular contributor.

Mike Peel wrote an extended piece for his club magazine the Blackheath Harriers Gazette dated 27th

September 1981 after his 2nd successful attempt in the London to Brighton Road Race in 7:03:29. A pretty quick time!

In the London Marathon's Media Guide for 2013 the EPs were given pride of place with their 2012 Marathon finishing statistics, a group photo and the quotation echoed in **Chapter 3 'A Disparate Group'**. *'They (the EPs) cover a whole spectrum of running backgrounds, come from all walks of life, different locations and assorted occupations, although many are now retired'*. Their non running lives are covered in **Chapter 9. 'Local Heroes'**

This curious story appeared in the Athletics Weekly in 1981 when more runners finished a race than started! It mentioned that in the 1981 Nike Peoples Marathon in Birmingham there were **1,858 starters** among whom were Jeff Aston and Dale Lyons, but they also recorded **1,900 finishers.** This conundrum was explained later in that it was due to an influx of unofficial runners! As a result 50 official finishers did not get a medal! Is this a first?

Guinness Worlds Records Annual

The fastest Egg & Spoon Marathon was recorded in the Guinness Book's 2012 edition under the heading *'Other Fast Finishes From the Wacky World of Sport'*. The citation read – *'Fastest Marathon with an Egg & Spoon, 3:47 Dale Lyons UK'*. Brief and to the point.

Chapter 7 Summary

Over the 33 years of the London Marathon an enormous amount of media coverage across the whole range has been dedicated to the EPs. Only a small selection of this range has been reviewed in this chapter but an effort has been made to include as many of the original 42 EPs as possible.

From radio and TV coverage to national and local newspapers, there have been poignant, humorous, amazing, sad and heart warming stories of the EPs going about their running business, usually in a self deprecating way.

The media coverage was due mainly to their status within the London Marathon, highlighting their running exploits and longevity. It was also due to the respect and admiration that has been accorded to those EPs who have achieved an amazing unbroken sequence of London Marathons.

The EPs link to a particular charity has also provided the media with an attractive human interest angle. In addition, the EPs occupation may have sparked a quirky news angle, as in the case of the hairdresser Charles Cousens. Or the attraction might have been because of a newly published book by Alastair Aitken. Or by the startling Bustard costume worn by Dale Lyons as reported in the Daily Mail.

Of course, our four EP Olympic Relay Torch carriers were certainly given the Full Monty on TV, radio and in their local newspapers. Their celebrity status was almost entirely due to their standing as EPs.

Whatever the reason, it is clear that as a group over many years, the EPs will continue to be a magnet for the media as they become better known. As the London Marathon grows into a grander annual spectacle the EPs will remain an integral part of its development and their attraction to the media.

CHAPTER 8

Ever-presents Charity Contributions
Introduction

Over the 33 years of the London Marathon the 27 EPs in this research have raised in the region of £250,000 for a variety of charities, organisations and individuals and for a mix of reasons. Some EPs have raised funds for many different charities while others have stuck to a single personal preference. The sums they have raised vary from a few hundred to many thousands of pounds.

The large organisations such as AgeUK draw in millions each year while others are grateful for donations of a few hundred as in the case of Animal Rescue Centres or local churches.

To get some idea of the growth of the London Marathon's charity involvement, their 2013 Media Guide provides evidence of the almost exponential surge in many aspects of the charity bandwagon.

Since 1981 over £600 million has been raised for the hundreds of charities that runners support each year and these charities were supported and sponsored by over 70% of London runners; an amazing percentage.

In 2010 the runners supporting the nominated London Charity CLIC Sargent raised in excess of £2 million. One can only imagine the frantic, hard nosed negotiations that take place before the Official London Charity is revealed each year when these sums are at stake.

The increase in support for charities is in part due to the introduction of the Gold Bond scheme by the London Marathon in 1993 whereby hundreds of charities were able to buy guaranteed entries for £300 and then *'sell'* them on for upwards of £1,500 to runners willing and able to raise the necessary sponsorship. It has to be said that Gold Bond numbers are limited and as such are eagerly sought after by the participating charities.

Doing *'good works'* is not restricted to these charities however because the London Marathon Ltd itself has its own charity, the London Marathon Charitable Trust. This charity has produced a surplus of almost £50 million which it has used to support over 1,000 projects, mainly sports related. Two key projects in this mix are the Playing Fields Scheme for the protection and purchase of vulnerable playing fields in London. The other is a £9 million grant for the Olympic Legacy Facilities after the 2012 London Games, by which seven sites have already been saved for the public. All the marathon runners can take due credit for these improved sports facilities in the capital.

This testimonial to the EPs was written by **Tom Wright CBE the Group Chief Executive of AgeUK,** one of the mainstream charities that was the London Marathon's official charity in 2013.

'For many people, successfully completing the London Marathon once is a hugely challenging feat. Having run the marathon myself, I'm well aware of the training, effort and physical toll that the London Marathon demands. To think that 15 members of the

group have run every London Marathon since the first event in 1981 is truly remarkable. The Everpresents act as a reminder to us all that age is just a number - not a barrier.'

A number of charitable categories have been used to separate areas of need below, in order to analyse the range and variety of the EPs contribution. Following these categories and the EPs involvement, a variety of thumbnail stories provide the reasons why the EPs supported the organisations they did.

Cancer *Cancer Research* UK Roger Mawer; Peter Greenwood; Steve Wehrle; Erik Falck-Therkelsen; *McMillan Nurses* Dale Lyons; Bryan Read; *Velindre Hospital* Jeff Aston; *Bobby Moore Fund* Dale Lyons; *Ovarian Cancer* Jeff Gordon.

Children *Run for Kids* David Clark; *NSPCC* Terry Macy; *Save the Children* Alastair Aitken; *Dreams come True* Steve Wehrle; *Action for the Crippled Child* Erik Falck-Therkelsen; *Great Ormond Street Hospital* Charles Cousens; *Action Aid* Rainer Burchett; *Homerton Hospital (premature babies)* Bill O'Connor:

Disabled *MS (Multiple Sclerosis)* Dave Clark;. *St.Mary's Kidney Hospital* Dave Fereday; *Muscular Dystrophy* Dale Lyons; *Hospital for Nervous Diseases* Alastair Aitken; *AgeUK* Dale Lyons; *Heart Foundation* Steve Wehrle; *Polio Plus* Dale Lyons;

Diabetes UK Erik Falk-Therkelsen;   *Cystic Fibrosis* Bryan Read..

Animal *Guide Dogs* Dave Clark;   *Save the Bustard* & *Solihull Animal Rescue* Dale Lyons.

Military *Help for Heroes* Chris Finill;   *RNLI* Erik Falck-Therkelsen.

Hospices *North London Hospice, St John's Hospice* Reg.Burbidge;   *Phyllis Tuckwell Hospice* Mike Peace; Chris Finill.

Humanitarian *Samaritans* Dave Clark;   *Oxfam* Mike Peel.

Mental Health *Scope (Cerebal Palsy)* Jan Hildreth;   *PSP (Palsy) Association* Bill O'Connor; *Alzheimers Trust* Dale Lyons;   *Parkinson's Disease* Peter Shepheard.

Local *Newbiggin Parish Church* Dave Fereday; *Church Repairs* Roger Mawer.

Ever-present charity stories

Over thirty institutions have been listed that the EPs have supported, not only with funds and help but with lots of attendant publicity in newspapers, on radio, in special events or roles within these institutions. Publicity is *'worth its weight in gold'* the charities will say and is often more valuable than donations, especially if an EP can be interviewed on BBC TV before, during or after the marathon and talk about their charity. So what are the reasons why the EPs supported the individuals, groups and organisations they did?

Bobby Moore was a hero to more than the footballing community and his early death from testicular cancer was an immense shock to the public at large. To honour his memory and to reduce deaths from this disease, Cancer Research UK created an offshoot, The Bobby Moore Fund. Dale Lyons, a football nut, decided to run the London Marathon in support of Bobby's fund and raised over £400.

For thirty years Action Aid have provided help for individual children and supported families to encourage their children to attend school. This is what attracted Rainer Burchett's support in the early years. More recently, Action Aid has extended its focus to concentrate additionally on aid to oppressed minorities in Third World countries through projects to increase self development. Rainer estimates he has raised £25,000 for Action Aid over the years.

Jeff Gordon was part of the Legal Charities group who decided to support the Ovarian Cancer charity using the considerable weight of the legal profession to generate funds and raise awareness.

On a smaller scale Roger Mawer's church was in need of repair to its clock tower so as a community member he rallied around to raise the necessary funds.

Dale Lyons took his two daughters to the Solihull Animal Sanctuary and realised how dedicated the staff were in caring for damaged and discarded animals on extremely limited resources, so he raised some badly needed funds for them.

Terry Macy decided to support abused children so he went out and raised £25,000 for their charity the NSPCC.

Because of the excellent treatment given to his two brothers by two local hospices Reg.Burbidge raised £3,000 for them which was sponsored by his London runs.

The Cardiff Post carried an article supporting Jeff Aston's charity sponsorship of the Cancer Research Unit at the Velindre Hospital where his sister works as a Ward Sister. The appeals co-ordinator John Burnett called Jeff's London record *"a tremendous achievement"* and his donation was used to improve facilities on the 1st Floor ward of the hospital.

Save the Children's charity sent a heartfelt thank-you letter to Erik Falck-Therkelsen for supporting the *'Famine in Africa Appeal'* and for his donation of £550.

For many years Dave Clark has supported his local MS society (Newbury & District Branch) with sponsorship from his London Marathons and a letter was sent to Dave with this message from Roy W Rayner, the ex President. *"Dave has most generously donated his sponsorship money raised by running in London Marathons to the branch. Over the years Dave (and Olive; Dave's wife) have become friends of the Society and without such people the branch would not exist in its current form. The branch owes a lot to*

Dave Clark and cannot praise him too highly". . High 5's for Dave and a good reason to keep him running!

Another personal reason motivated Erik Falck-Therkelsen to raise funds for the Diabetes UK because his wife is a diabetic.

A similar reason for raising funds over many years through his London Marathon for SCOPE, the Cerebral Palsy charity was because Jan Hildreth's son suffered from the same condition. Subsequently he became their Honorary Treasurer.

David Walker sponsored Cancer Research and the British Heart Foundation because of his parent's death from cancer and a heart attack. He also supported Asthma Relief because of a childhood illness. For another charity, the Ian Rennie Hospice at Home, David became a sponsor and a main speaker for their Gold Bold scheme.

On a slightly contentious note, Mike Wilkinson had raised funds for many years for a charity but stopped supporting them when they raised the amount runners had to collect for a Gold Bond marathon entry.

Charles Cousens has sponsored the Great Ormond Street Hospital for sick children and in October 2013 they were delighted to send him a fund-raising certificate for his help over sixteen years and for the £8,637 he has donated over that period and a signed *'thank you'* card from the children – see a copy in the media credits section.

A disabled friend required a stair lift in his house but funds were not available so Bryan Read ran the London and raised £400 to help install the lift. Then, to help send Bryan to the New York Marathon his disabled students raised £200. As a result he raised the grand sum of £6,000 for Macmillan Nurses. What a marvellous return on their investment!

London Marathon sponsors 1981 - 2013

Without the funding of the London by major organisations it could not have survived to grow into a global marathon heavyweight.   See **appendix 9 Marathon Sponsors 1981 – 2013**

The following six organisations have not only kept the London Marathon afloat over the past 33 years but they have made a significant contribution to the Marathon's world ranking status and with help to top the league of charitable donations worldwide.

Gillette, the razor multinational, sponsored the first London and said they were very pleased with the increased exposure for their investment of £78,000 for the first year of their three year contract.

Next into the breach was the confectioner **Mars** who signed up for £150,000 rising to £250,000 until 1988, which meant the Marathon was a well and truly established attraction to the international market movers and shakers.

By 1989 the Marathon was an international publicity magnet with six more organisations competing to be the London Marathon's official charity. The amount of sponsorship donated was not revealed by the winner, **ADT** security systems but their financial clout did help to attract the IAAF World Marathon Cup in 1991.   The London was now a world ranking institution.

From 1993 to 1995 **Nutrasweet,** the low calorie sweetener helped to bring new levels of administrative professionalism to the Marathon, resulting in record entry levels and a spectacular finish at Buckingham Palace.

Flora the poly-unsaturates giant became the longest running sponsor from 1996 to 2009, heralding the boom in charity donations to world record levels in which naturally, the EPs played an important part. These developments established the London as one of the five World Marathon Majors along with New York, Boston, Chicago and Berlin.

Finally, in 2010 Richard Branson's **Virgin Money** introduced an increased professionalism to charity funding by their non-profit website *'Virgin Money Giving'* ramping up their donations to a five year high of £250,000.

These six big hitters were backed up by many key secondary sponsors with household names like **Adidas, Timex, Lucozade Sport** and **Nestle Pure Life** who supply the crucial water and carbohydrate drinks to the runners.

The international prestige and variety of these companies provide clear evidence from their own admission that there was a significant marketing cost-benefit advantage for whatever sums they donated to the Marathon's coffers. Over the 33 years of London the hundreds of thousands of Marathon medals have been engraved with the names of these sponsors generating a significant publicity boost.

Each year the EPs have done their bit by flying the flag with the Marathon sponsors logos on their **'I've run every London'** 'T' shirts.

The EPs are now a part of the marathon *'extravaganza'* and add to the human interest stories which attract the attention of the media and make the London very special diary date each year.

Chapter 8 Summary

Were the EPs driven to run the London Marathon in order to support needy organisations or was this used as a justification for their primary aim of wanting to be part of a great city marathon? It seems clear from the evidence that the EP's primary aim, was to run and in the process serve a wholly laudable and altruistic end result in raising badly needs funds for the charities they wanted to support.

Another reason was to be a part of a gradually increasing mass movement for the London to be seen to be more than just a national spectacle each year but to serve as a burgeoning tourist attraction

Whatever the reason or justification for the present day London the EPs have satisfied these aims to a remarkable degree. By raising huge sums for good causes across the charity spectrum and at the same time making sure their presence has added to the Marathon's growth as an annual extravaganza. The EPs have played no small part in this process.

CHAPTER 9

Local Heroes

Ever-presents non-marathon lives

Introduction
The titles given to each of the EPs in this chapter relate either to their profession, sporting interest or place of birth and it is clear that EPs come from all walks of professions and industries. Their ages range widely too, from the mid 50's to the high 70's, with Reg. Burbidge, well into his ninth decade at 88! The twenty-seven contributors to the research are represented in the personal thumbnail sketches that follow.

Every EP's family and local culture informs their non-sporting interests, education and associations. Some have extended families as most are now well into retirement and some are even great-grand parents. Many of the EPs have passed on their interests and genes to the next generation into running marathons and even ultras and perhaps this is not surprising. Some of the wives, partners and siblings are also marathon runners.

Many have stuck with their club affiliations to provide management and coaching skills while others have extended their life skills into community projects and services. Others have been happy to help out their offspring by tending grand-children and, in the process thoroughly enjoying the experience.

Their recreational interests cover a wide spectrum of activities too, from gardening and yoga to painting and musicianship, from wine appreciation to theatre visits. There is little common thread in these varied pursuits. The EPs, after all are just your average human beings, apart that is from their ability to run very long distances over many, many years!

The Author

Another one of our Scotsmen, Alastair Aitken was born in the City of Edinburgh then moved nearer to the British capital in Norwood, South West London. Alastair is an author of some distinction with three books to his credit, the most recent being '*Running Enigmas*'.

He has been married for 41 years to Joanna a qualified physiotherapist, now a theatre agent. They have a son Andrew who is also a fast runner with a 1:15, half marathon and a Rotterdam Marathon time of 2:50 to his credit.

Initially Alastair wanted to become a journalist so he passed some shorthand and typing exams at Pitmans College and even won the Pitmans half mile race. At seventeen he wrote his first article for the house journal but still could not break into journalism. With his authorship of three sporting books however, he obviously had the potential.

His next option for the day job was an Insurance Claims Broker at Hogg Robinson in the City lasting 32 years and finally on a part-time basis for RFIB. He is now retired aged 73 and can now divert his attention to more relaxing pursuits such as writing articles for the club magazine at Highgate Harriers where his is the editor.

Some of his recreational interests sound exciting with horse racing (spectating only) at the Cheltenham Festival and as a long term member of the Frank Sinatra Appreciation Society with a collection of 72 albums. To top it all he is also a committed Miles Davis jazz fanatic so without doubt, Alastair leads a full and rewarding life.

The Aussie

Born down-under in the town of Lock, Victoria, Rainer Burchett now aged 74, left Australia when only three years old and after a year in India came to the UK. The reason for all this travelling was that his father was a War Correspondent who convalesced in India after being wounded in Burma while covering Orde Wingate's campaign in the Far East.

His father, Wilfred Burchett was also the first Western journalist to visit Hiroshima shortly after the atomic bomb was dropped there. Rainer was not very happy decamping to England in 1943 because in 1944 he was bombed out by the Luftwaffe and had to be evacuated to Derbyshire.

He has been married for 42 years to Doreen who was born in Hackney and they have two daughters, one of whom, Judith, has run six Londons, one with Dad. Helen, the other daughter is not keen on running.

After grammar school and a degree in History at Cambridge, he formed a successful business for twenty years which was floated on stock-markets in the UK and America. Not content with one degree he then completed a part-time economics degree at the LSE, in 1960.

His is now retired after 21 years in business and since then has completed another degree in maths and physics at the OU (Open University) and is now working on an OU Masters degree in Classical Civilisation, not an easy option. By the sound of it Rainer is a confirmed student.

He still finds plenty of time for his other interests in music, opera and fine wine (drinking); one of his favourites being Chateau Palmer, a Grande Cru Classe Bordeaux from the Haut Medoc (but don't call it claret!).

Rainer's take on the profile of an EP is a varied one but thinks *"we must all share some sort of dogged determination to keep going no matter what"*.

The Consultant

Peter Shepheard is another Scot, born in Dunfermline but now lives in Bromley, Kent where he lives with his wife Barbara of 40 years. Like Peter, she is a runner and has completed three London, seven behind his daughter Hazel with ten so Londons obviously *'run'* in the family.

He retired after 30 year with Lloyds Bank in the City as a Financial Services Consultant to concentrate on his stamp and record collection, having been a DJ in an earlier life.

At 70 and still a confirmed running junkie he now supports his daughter and son-in-law in their races.

The Director–General

Jan Hildreth was born on the Isle of Wight and during his school-days became the Head Boy at Wellington College. After graduating from Queens College, Oxford he joined the Royal Artillery's 44th Parachute Brigade from 1953 to 1958 as a paratrooper before embarking on a varied and glittering career.

Perhaps the pinnacle among his many societal roles was to become the Director General of the Institute of Directors, a role he was well qualified for after senior management positions with Shell Oil and as a finance guru on the Board of London Transport. He then turned his financial acumen to help develop the Textile and Wool trade by serving on their NEDDIE (National Economic Development Executive) in the 1970's.

If you want to read the *'Full Monty'* of Jan's illustrious career you will find the detail in '**Who's Who**' under his name, **Henry Jan Hamilton Crossley Hildreth!**

Married for many years, Jan and Wendy had two sons, Gerald, Gavin and a daughter Francis before embarking on their pastime of cottage renovation. Their first in Wiltshire was shortly followed by another in Windrush, Oxfordshire which they bought for £1,500 and then finally they renovated a water mill in Dartmoor, restoring it to pristine condition. DIY specialists or what?

More recently, in 2010 Jan became Chairman of *'The Castle'* climbing wall which was an old water pumping station previously used to train fireman and finally restored under his tutelage as a local community facility.

The Doctor

Although Tunbridge Wells is his hometown, Doc Mac Speake trained as a GP at Leeds University for five years then served time in Leeds and Bradford hospitals. Now a youthful 71 and retired as a GP after thirty two years, he has settled in Kettlebaston, a delightful village in Norfolk.

He is married to Ros and has a rather large extended family of one daughter, three sons and six grandchildren i.e. four boys and two girls. All of his children and even a daughter-in-law are hooked on running having done a raft of Londons and triathlons (half and full Ironman no less). This family involvement helps Mac retain his EP status, by keeping his fitness up to scratch.

Mac tells a holiday story with his wife in a South of France Chambre d'Hote (B & B), not dissimilar he said, to a Transylvania castle, where the hosts supplied a very meagre meal and carried on shouting and fighting all night. Mac said *"we locked ourselves in the room and couldn't get out fast enough the next morning!"*

The European

David Walker is another displaced Scot from Paisley but left there as an infant and decamped to Farnborough in Hampshire.

He now lives in Chesham Buckinghamshire with his wife Lin to whom he has been married for 43 years. David has passed down his motivation to run to their three children, clearly demonstrated when they all ran the London with him.

His children have in fact run a bewildering number of Londons with Jamie twice, Hannah three times and John, nine. Even David's daughter-in-law Lisa has run five Londons, the latest in 2010. Not to be outdone however, his wife Lin completed the tough London Moonwalk.

Before retiring in 2005 aged 67, David was the Director of Learning and Development for EAMER (European, Africa and Middle Eastern Region). He has still kept his educational irons in the fire by setting up his own executive coaching business and career advisor service in local Job Centres. In addition, he volunteers his consultancy skills at the College of North West London by mentoring youngsters in trouble at school and with the police.

Some of David's spare non-running time is taken up with the London Welsh Rugby Male Voice Choir where, on the Lions tour in 2005 they sang on the New Zealand TOTP (top of the pops).

With the rest of his time David finds his recreation on a weekly basis taken up with three grandkids, Rosie 4, Sammy 12 months and the newest arrival Olive 6 months. Although he confesses that *"this seems a bit boring I just love being a grandpa, and our three little ones are such a joy"*. Obviously a grandad to cherish!

The Fireman

For 30 years Ray Johnson served in the Nottingham Fire & Rescue Service and gives them full credit for providing the impetus for kick-starting his love of running.

His family have taken a lead from Ray's running exploits with his wife Barbara taking up the London baton with three circuits. Not to be outdone, his daughter Hazel has completed ten Londons and is still a competitive runner. It must be in the genes you know.

Ray has featured in local papers and on Midlands TV for his marvellous record of 27 Londons and has been dubbed the *'Galloping Grandad'*. Just to show he was not past it after relinquishing his EP status in 2007 with gout, he ran the 2009 London and *"felt OK"*.

The Fitness Coach

A true Cockney by birth, born in Bow, East London, Bryan Read has stayed that side of London. He is now an Essex Boy living happily in a cottage in Blackmore, a small village in Essex with his wife Vera of 51 years. Both his children Nicola 45 and Grant 43 are long distance runners, showing their Dad he is not the only runner in the family.

For 18 years Bryan was a school teacher at Upton House in Hackney and then for 35 years, the Head of P.E. in Special Education at Hayley House School helping young people with behavioural problems.

For his skill and dedication in helping these children Bryan was awarded a National Lifetime Award in 2003, against stiff opposition, at a gala presentation in Cambridge. The award, Bryan said *"came out of the blue!"*

Some of his spare time is taken up with honing the football skills of London Boys under 18 team at Eton Manor. With the remainder of his time he runs circuit training classes as a volunteer for teenagers, on a weekly basis. Not surprisingly, Bryan still finds time to coach under 10 footballers every week in the season - *"West Ham United wannabees"* jokes Bryan.

The Grandad

Now 88 years young Reg. Burbidge was born in the East End of London where he still lives. Reg is now a widower but has a very large family of fifteen, made up of two sons and a daughter, six grandchildren and **six great grandchildren** to keep him on his toes. What an inheritance Reg!

Before retiring he was for many years a LGO (Local Government Officer) working for the GLC.

Reg still weight trains at the local gym and mixes this up with long walks, watching cricket in the season and spectating at the local athletics meetings near his home in North London.

The Hairdresser

Although Charles Cousens was born in Tring Harfordshire he has since spent many blissful years in Suffolk near Lowestoft. He still giving short back and sides and more exotic cuts in his family's hairdressing salon where he was trained as a fifteen year old by his father.

Married for 45 years to Maureen another 3:30 marathoner and one son Lee 44 who doesn't run, he is an inveterate hoarder. He has spent almost 40 years collecting military memorabilia, especially bayonets, and now, Charles says he has a *"room full"*

In 2011 he was invited to Birmingham's prestigious ICC (International Convention Centre) to give an hour speech to an audience of hundreds on keeping fit, a subject that he was well equipped to deliver, being an EP with the relevant background and skills set. Apparently, the Birmingham audience loved it.

The Head Teacher

For 27 happy years Mike Peace kept a tight rein on his pupils at Frimley Junior School for Surrey County Council and only retired this year, still a youthful 64. Prior to his present home in Farnborough Hampshire where he has lived for many years Mike was born and raised in Hoyland, a coal mining village near Barnsley and is *"fiercely proud of it."*

After being divorced after 9 years he joined his present partner Annie and together they have a houseful of eight children, with three boys and a girl each. It must be fun at meal-times.

With Mike as a shining example to the benefits of running, three have taken up the sport with his old club Ranelagh Harriers. Joseph and Jacob compete in the sub marathon distances up to 10 miles with Chris showing the way in the marathon, running his first London in a very respectable 4:01 in 2012. Mike is rightly proud of his running brood.

The Industrialist

Dave Fereday, born in London's Muswell Hill, is an astute businessman, running the family owned company H.Fereday & Sons, (est. 1862) from his base in Tyneside. They are makers of high quality Caterlux hot-cupboards and Weylux scales for the catering industry and sell world-wide.

For recreation Dave regularly digs up his two allotments in which he grows all the family's vegetables and often wins the Borough prize for the best kept allotment. He is also a family man, married to Alison for fifteen years and with three children by his first wife they are all are *'runners of a sort'* according to Dave.

Peter, his son, ran the Birmingham marathon when almost an infant at the age of thirteen in 4:30, the Abingdon in 3:50 and at seventeen ran the Bedford Marathon in his fastest time of 2:51. but then gave up! What wasted potential!

His other son Michael is a keen recreational runner and his daughter Wendy ran the London in 1991 at the age of twenty five. Dave has obviously passed on some of his running abilities to his children.

The Kiwi

A Kiwi by birth from Greymouth in New Zealand's South Island, Bill O'Connor now lives in Finchley, North London. His brother is a missionary priest in Pakistan who is also a cracking runner, coming second in the 1984 Pakistan Marathon in a blistering 2:21. Obviously, running is in the family.

Bill has been married since 1974 to Patricia and they have four daughters Kathryn, Margaret, Patricia and Marie two of whom live in Australia.

Bill's first class performances seem to run in his family with his sister Mary 2nd to World renowned marathoner Grete Waitz (World Champion) in 1983 and 1986. Joan Benoit an Olympic Champion was only two places ahead of Marie in the 1986 world rankings. Marie was also 3rd ranked marathon runner in 1984, representing New Zealand for nineteen years and winning medals galore. She also ran for the Kiwis in the Olympic and Commonwealth games. What an amazing sibling!

His New Zealand father joined the Anzac forces during the 2nd World War in the 23rd and 26th Battalions and were part of the successful El Alamien and North Africa desert campaigns in 1940. After fighting in Tobruk, Bengazi and Tunis he was seriously injured in the arm and two weeks later Rommel's Axis forces were defeated. A family history to treasure.

After 50 enjoyable years as a teacher Bill has been at Queens Park Community (Secondary) School with 1,200 pupils since 1989 and is still going strong.. At 68 he is also involved in running, as President of the Children Cross Country League, the largest in the UK with 1,000 participants.

Bill also keeps the funds in order as treasurer of the North London Cross Country Association and serves on the committees of North Thames Cross Country League and West London Athletic Network in his other day job.

He is still an active member of Queens Park Harriers where he has held every committee role over the years and is still officiating as Cross Country Captain, Treasurer and Membership Secretary. A clubman par excellence!

The Lawyer

Jeff Gordon started in the legal profession as a bright 16 year old and now at 79 has 63 years in public funded legal work behind him.

Another illustrious honour for Jeff was to become the Legal Aid Lawyer for 2003 due to his persistence in supporting clients who were refused legal aid, one of whom was a West Indian dustman, Levene Mackensie. Eventually this action brought in the *'Mackensie Support'*, a system providing legal aid and now enshrined in statute law. During his tenure as a lawyer

Jeff was an acquaintance of the Lord Chief Justice, Peter Taylor.

A more sobering feature of Jeff's public involvement was his twelve failed attempts to be the Conservative candidate in the local elections. He has however, been an Independent Councillor and a very active politician for 30 years!

A more recent highlight of Jeff Gordon's running career was to be selected in 2012 for the Olympic Torch Relay through the streets of London's Wandsworth on July 23$^{rd.}$ He then handed the torch over to a *'nice'* Tim Henman, the tennis star

Jeff was born in London's East End, Hackney but for the last forty years has lived in Putney with his second wife Shirley, a qualified hypnotherapist and previously a dancer on pop shows.

She is also Queen Ratling, the female equivalent of King Rat, the Water-Rats fund raising entertainers charity. Another claim to fame for Shirley was, as a 12 year old she went to school with Barbara Windsor (Carry On films) and Shirley Eaton (the Bond girl in Goldfinger). A wife to cherish.

The Marathon Man

Without doubt 176 is a lot of marathons, a statement on which Peter Greenwood would agree because they total over 4,600 miles!

Peter was born in Blackpool but decided to move to Whitstable the oyster capital of England. He is single with three sons, two of whom have completed the London with him.

Peter was a Quality Assurance Manager before retiring at 71 and as part of his recreational activities he loves classical music.

The Master Chef

Dale Lyons is an ex pat Geordie from North Shields, Tyne & Wear and for his sins can't help supporting Newcastle United aka The Magpies. One of his claims to fame is that he went to the same school in Whitley Bay as Dick Clements and Ian Le Frenais the creators of the TV series *'The Likely Lads'*.

He first trained as a Master Chef at London's top hotel, The Connaught. He then heard the call of HRH and with other National Service *'volunteers'* was conscripted into the RAF. This was *"The best time of my life"* said Dale, where he escaped the customary parades as an Officers Mess Chef and then played football for the Bomber Command HQ's team, at the same time collecting his Catering Management qualifications

After his RAF demob he emigrated to the USA and did the rounds in New York and Pennsylvania as a chef, a Motor Inn Restaurant Manager, a Food Ops. Manager at New York's 1963 Worlds Fair, a *'Good Humor Man'* selling ice cream and anything else that paid the rent.

On his return to the UK Dale moved into group catering management but teaching and lecturing in Higher Education and with the Open University looked a better option. With a BA and an M.Sc in his pocket he settled into college management as a Head of

Department and Marketing Director at Birmingham's renowned College of Food before retiring to start his own consultancy in 1989.

In between times he has been a College Inspector for BTEC and toured the world as a BESO (British Executive Service Overseas) and VSO volunteer developing catering and educational facilities in Nepal, Ukraine, Estonia, China and Slovakia.

Now retired at 76, he spent some time playing saxes in two big bands and now plucks the banjo in the Midlands Fretted Orchestra. For additional pleasure he plays clarinet in a R & B group and thrashes around local golf courses with little sign of improvement.

Dale wrote his autobiography in 2012 and also writes tongue in cheek marathon reports after each London. See **appendix 8 LM Report 2003,** the year Chris Brasher died.

Family-wise he is twice divorced and lives an idyllic life with his partner Janet in leafy Edgbaston, Birmingham. Janet considers him *'obsessive'* in regards to the marathon but is still an ardent on course London groupie every April.

Dale has two daughters, Kyla, who ran the London Marathon in 1985 and Iona a homoeopath, both of whom ran the Great North Run to keep him company. With four grand-kids Joe, Marisa, Anna and Niamh, the youngest, Dale is kept on the ball.

The Media Man

Steve Wehrle was born in Paddington but moved to the rural attractiveness of Orpington, in Kent and lives there with his wife Ann whom he married in 1998. They have a 21 year old son Matthew who has run a half marathon and intends to train as an RAF pilot.

Before his job for life, Steve studied at Wandsworth Tech and then worked for 48 years as a Production Manager, initially for the BBC and then a satellite company, Immediate Media. Allied to the BBC, Steve established the BBC Running Club 30 years ago which he helped to develop into an in-house institution.

For his first claim running club, the Dulwich Runners he served in almost every club responsibility up to the role of Chairman. Obviously a Clubman extraordinaire.

For fun and recreation Steve holds an enviable collection of pop albums from the 50's to 70's including a cache of Beatles memorabilia. He also practices yoga and helps young musicians in Orpington by promoting their concerts with his skills honed by his years in the media business.

The Radioman

David Clark is another EP Scot who left his ancestral home for the bright lights in the Home Counties of Berkshire. Married for 56 years to his wife Olive they have two sons Martin and John plus three grandchildren, two girls and one boy. Unfortunately, none has shown David's predilection for running.

On the work scene David served as a cycle engineer for four years after studying at a building college. He then joined the Royal Navy and trained as an AB (Able Seaman) Telegrapher and Morse code.

After leaving the Royal Navy he spent six years at Bush Radio as a TV and Radio technician and another six working for Microfocus Software before retiring in 2010. A very varied work life indeed.

Dave did not embark on running until he was 39 and then only after trying a fun run and deciding *"I found that I was not too bad at it!"* He didn't look back after that.

His hobbies include walking and oil painting, at which David is a dab hand. *"I've dozens of them so I usually donate them to the family"* said David. I'll bet they're really pleased with his largesse.

The Running Man

Chris Finill was born in Harrow Middlesex 54 years ago in the same road as running legend Roger Bannister. He now lives in Cranleigh, Surrey and says part of the enjoyment of the London is having family support with Julia his wife, cheering him on for thirty two years. Could she be considered an ex gratia female Ever-present, Chris wonders? Not satisfied with watching, Julia decided to run the London in 2010 in celebration her 50th birthday! That's the way to show them!

Chris's son Tom and daughter Jo also ran the London in 2007 and 2009 both when eighteen, almost in nappies, and his youngest Nick now twenty, is under some family pressure to perform likewise.

Employment-wise, Chris trained as a Chartered Accountant in 1986 and is still practising his financial skills as the Bursar at the prestigious Duke of Kent School in Surrey.

When not running Chris Finill spends his time travelling and has a keen interest in photography.

The Skier

Erik Falck-Therkelsen is our only ex-pat Norwegian who came to England to work as a Broker on the Baltic Exchange from 1967 until 1985 leaving his cross country skis behind. After he tired of the City of London life he decamped to Woking Borough Council as an LGO (Local Government Officer) in 1987 doing highway surveys and landscaping on a part-time basis.

Erik is now a very fit 72 but still finds lots of time for his highways work. Based on his in-depth knowledge of countryside maintenance Erik turned his skills to restoring the Basingstoke canal locks in Surrey as a volunteer. This long work in progress kept him busy for eight years until it re-opened in 1988 and a job well done for the public to enjoy.

He has been married to Susan for longer than he can remember but having a daughter aged 41 and a son aged 37 will give you some idea. They are all still mightily impressed with his London Marathon EP record of 21 completions.

Once he has sorted some niggling health problems from which he hopes to make a full recovery, Erik said *"I very much look forward to 3 to 6 miles of gentle running through familiar Surrey countryside"*. We'll all drink to that Erik!

The Solicitor
Job-wise, Terry Macy still has his nose to the employment grindstone at 67, having been self employed as a solicitor for forty years.

Born in the cathedral city of Canterbury and now living near Blackheath, Terry is divorced but with the bonus of a son and daughter.

Following in his footsteps, his daughter Rebecca has run two Londons and the Chicago Marathon with him. His son Derrick ran the Nottingham half marathon recently with Terry in a little over two hours.

He is by far the nearest EP to the London Marathon Green start (about 400 yards!), living as he does on Shooters Hill Road, Blackheath.

The Systems Man
Apart from his running, Jeff Aston still finds time for walking holidays, researching his family's history, gardening, classical music and cooking. His favourite dish is Steak Casserole in Red Wine but the dessert that he gets high fives for is his Lemon Tart. Mmmmh!

Currently he is acting as a house husband doing the cooking, cleaning and other household chores in order to give his wife Val, a nurse who he has been married to for 26 years, a well earned break..

Jeff has passed on some of his running genes to his daughter Emma who has run two Londons but his other Amy has not yet caught the bug. With three grandchildren, Connor, Cole and Kaci, there is still enough potential in the extended family to carry on the running tradition.

When not on grand-parenting duties Jeff enjoys spending time researching the family history in order to see how many skeletons he can unearth.

On the business side, Jeff retired after twenty three years with Rockwell, a Danish company specialising in IT Support as a Systems Analyst.

The Ultra Man

Mike Wilkinson was born in Ipswich and not far from where he now lives in Norwich. But which Norfolk team does he support, Ipswich or Norwich? Mike has a record size family with 3 sons, 4 grandchildren, **2 great grandchildren,** and he is still only 75!

As a teenager he played hockey and rugby union, the latter as a Norfolk Colt until employment beckoned. Job-wise he started off as a quantity surveyor then joined the Royal Navy as a Victualler with the rank of Petty Officer after failing to become a Fleet Air Arm pilot. During his service Mike was *'put on a fizzer'* (reprimanded) for running around the deck of an aircraft carrier to keep fit. The ship's Captain was not amused.

Leaving the Navy Mike became an international insurance brokerage, then after two years in college he joined Norwich City Council in financial services for 13 years, at the age of 50

Chris, his youngest is a hockey player, but runs competitively on occasion, in fact good enough to beat Mike in half marathon races. Another son Andrew, ran the Ipswich 10 mile in a speedy 1:07 when only ten years old. Some potential or what?

Another of Mike's extra-curricula pursuits involves researching his family tree and what dark secrets he discovered about his maternal grandmother. Born in 1886, she bore five children then ran off with a soldier, had a further five children by the soldier, only to commit suicide in 1937, at the age of 51. Having discovered the other side of his grandmother's family, he was delighted eventually to meet some of her children.

He still turns out for the annual Norwich half Marathon, organised by his club the City of Norwich AC where he has Membership Number 1 and was race director 30 years earlier.

Mike still feels part of the EP culture especially for the camaraderie and from 2008 he has been at the Green Start come rain or shine to support the EPs, now with his wife Eileen who unfortunately has Alzheimer's. They both have a good time making their way around the course spotting and cheering on the EPs.

The Web Master

Mike Peel has been the President of Blackheath & Bromley Harriers as well as Delaune CC and still retains the working title of *'The Steward'*. *"Looking after the club's premises and cleaning the toilets!"* says Mike, as well as their website naturally.

He was born in Beckenham, Kent and still lives close by in Bromley so he has not drifted far in his 71 years. Mike is a divorcee but now lives with his partner Terri who has caught his running bug, having completed several Londons. His two sons Mark, 44 and Andrew 42 have not followed in Mike's running footsteps despite his good example.

Mike started his work-life as a draughtsman then ended up in insurance on the computer side. When he started in the mid sixties he reckons there were only four computers in the whole of London! Hard to believe.

His real claim to fame was in 2012 when he was selected from thousands for his services to charity and his EP status, to run in the Olympic Torch Relay near Crystal Palace. Fortunately the weather was glorious for his 400 yards dash through the packed ranks of spectators, family and friends.

On the recreational side he enjoys photography and on computers he is a whizz of course. Mike even built a kit-car 25 years ago and can still be seen bombing around the Kent countryside adorned with goggles and helmet.

The Welshman

At home in Bally, Wales, Mick McGeoch lives only 200 yards from his birthplace and last year he celebrated his Silver Wedding anniversary to his sweetheart Caroline whom he met in the local pub. As a mark of respect for this auspicious occasion he even shaved off his beard. What a sacrifice Mick!

His gainful employment for the past 21 years been as a Hospital Administrator for the NHS where he closely audits clinical standards of care. He also writes for his club magazine ACE, mentors young running hopefuls and even finds time to do some public speaking, naturally on running topics.

He is still running enthusiastically at the youthful age of 58 with sessions at his club, Les Croupiers.

The Yachtsman

Roger Mawer was born in Lyndhurst a small village in the New Forest although he was raised in Gosport, Hampshire where he developed his interest in sailing. He now lives in Norwich and worked for 22 years as a jobbing gardener, retiring in his early 70's due to a debilitating illness.

His three sons were encouraged to run and all have completed the London and were equally successful in their careers. One is an architect, another a helicopter pilot for the Army Air Force and the third an eye surgeon. A proud father no doubt!

The Yankee

Our only American EP, Roger Low was born in the USA in Alabama then moved to Wisconsin as his father was a US Army Captain in the medical corps. Roger followed a similar career path as a US Marine when in his 20s after which he attended a University of Pennsylvania graduate programme at Wharton School in Philadelphia. Moving to the UK in 1972, he became a stock broker until 2008 and currently he works part-time as an Investor Relations Consultant at Phoenix Investor Relations.

Roger has been married to author, Helen Bryan, for 46 years and they have two children. Now, at 69 he spends his leisure time skiing in France, Italy and the Rockies as well as doing a good job as a part-time minder to his two grand-children.

Roger thinks his psychological profile is *"driven; able to concentrate and focus; willing to accept hardship, pain, heat, cold; (and is) a loner"* He certainly related to a NYC Marathon spectator sign which read. *."If you are still married, you aren't training hard enough!"* Isn't that the truth?

Chapter 9 Summary

A heading for this Chapter gave the EPs the title *'Local Heroes'* and it can be seen that through each of these greatly abbreviated thumbnail summaries of their professional and home life there is ample evidence to support that title. They all gave, and are giving something back to their communities, in a variety of ways.

For example we have four who have brought national recognition to their areas with the Olympic Torch Relay, while others have won prestigious recognition for their work in and for the community.

At a local level many have been and still are engaged in projects to enhance and help the lives of young men and women. Some have passed on their experience in sports and running at public conferences or in musical performances.

Apart from running, the EPs have been a credit to their communities in many different ways and over many years, just take a look at their charity contributions in **Chapter 8**.for example.

The EPs families, friends, and clubmen I am sure would agree with the title of '*local heroes*', and not only because of their London Marathon exploits.

CHAPTER 10

A Future for Ever-presents or a Diminishing Breed?

Introduction

At the outset of the research for this book the anticipated sample was 50% i.e. 20 of the remaining 39 EPs. In the event this was exceeded for active EPs with 87% (13) and with non-active EPs 52% (14) an overall sample size of almost 70% (27), well above expectations. The detailed responses from the surveys and the follow-up phone calls, e-mails and mailings allowed a good depth of qualitative and quantitative information on a range of topics (**see appendix 2 Research Survey**).

Once the EPs realised the book was to be written and read the first chapters, they warmed to the task and more information and detail flooded in for the later chapters.

A question still remains as to the variation in the original EP numbers and this issue was raised in the first chapter. One letter from the London Marathon stated that 41 EPs had been approved in 1995 and not 42. The contributing EPs were counselled as to this quandary but no compelling evidence was produced.

A possible answer to this conundrum could be that in 1995 when computer analysis and data was less sophisticated, digging out these EPs from the many thousands of finishers was inexact at best. This was also compounded by the fact that runners had to provide proof to the London Marathon of their 15 year continuity and that had to be matched to the computerised results. This was further complicated as some EP's ran under other names but were subsequently admitted under 'fast for age' rules.

Despite all this confusion it seems a reasonable assumption that everyone who should have been given the good news of their EP status in 1995 was given it.

Who will be the Last Ever-present?

Which EP will have the crowning achievement of being the last one to run in the London Marathon? Well, at the present rate of 1.5 EPs annual wastage and with 15 still remaining it will be around 2022 before we find out. But, on whom does the best money lie to be that last man? If age is the main determinant then it won't be Ken (Jones) or Jeff (Gordon), both on 79, or even Dale (Lyons) at 76. For the remainder there are four more in their 70's and seven still in their 60's but the *'baby'* by far and leading the rest by ten years is Chris (Finill) at 54. He has to be the overwhelming favourite, but does he?

Some dropped off the EP perch by accident and not by age or infirmity, remember Alastair Aitken's horrendous accident. But how many ways are there to fall off this perch? Well, EPs no longer have to wait and see if they are lucky in the marathon lottery. Does illness and injury intervene? Maybe, but one EP stalwart has organised both knee and ankle replacements during the off season so that the London stays on his agenda. The same head-case broke a hip training for an Ironman event and got round a few months later on crutches.

Not a few EP's have ran with broken bones, pulled muscles, various levels of sickness and even on crutches over the years. Shuffling off the mortal coil seems to be the most likely excuse but it would not surprise anyone if they were not nailed back on the perch like a 'Monty Python' parrot! See the cartoon in the media credits.

At the birth of the EPs the 2nd youngest and fastest was Mick (McGeoch) who succumbed to an achilles injury in a 10 mile race shortly before the 2003 London which put paid to his EP status. Ironically, he carried on **after** the 2003 lapse to complete another seven Londons.

There are no guarantees however for anyone to continue as an EP but if the present fifteen can avoid illness, injury, accident, death and the other countless ways of preventing them from starting or completing the London then they stand as good as chance as anyone of standing alone on the top of the mountain. It's long odds on many of them making it to 2022 on the evidence to hand. Still, the smart money must be on Chris when all said and done.

Geoff Wightman the international marathoner (2:13) and organiser of the London Marathon finish line for twenty two years makes this very point about the EPs'. *"It is an unbelievable achievement - just getting to the start for all those years is difficult enough"*.

What have we learned about the Ever-presents?

Most, if not all the EPs active and non-active would agree they were lucky to get into the first London Marathon in 1981. Some were entered on the 2nd bite of the cherry, after running with someone else's number, normally a disqualification offence. See the **appendices 3 and 4** 1995 letters saying there were only 41 EPs.

For some it was their first marathon and they were uncertain as to whether they would last the distance. From the EPs comments over the years, either due to injury, fatigue or other reasons, many would have registered a DNS or even a DNF if they had not been current EPs as it was their over-riding motivation to maintain the sequence that kept them going. Witness many of the current EP's quotes to that effect in **chapters 3 and 4.**

We have learned that all bar five EPs have looked abroad for bigger and better challenges. Just refer to **Chapter 5 'Globetrotters'** to see the amazing mix of countries and distances the EPs have travelled in their search for the ultimate marathon or ultra. While on their travels all of them have acquitted themselves with some style as UK or England representatives.

While it could be said that running was the prime motivation for their international travels it can be seen that there were other factors involved such as *'voyages of discovery'* and altruism. They had an almost neo-colonial need to spread the often denigrated word of

'*Britishness*', with many proudly wearing the Union Jack on their running gear. Supporting many charities and other groups was a clear indication of their altruism both by example and sponsorship, and often for very personal reasons; as detailed in **Chapter 8 Charities**.

What comes across in **Chapter 6 Media** is the EPs' constant motivation to improve themselves both as runners and role models. Whether this was for PBs (personal bests), or to be seen winning or surviving in the face of steep odds, at a club, county, country or international level.

The London Marathon Media Guide for 2013 listed six London objectives initially drawn up by Chris Brasher and John Disley when they founded the Marathon back in 1981. Four of these would clearly apply to the EPs in serving London's mission over the years.

1. 'To show to mankind that, on occasions, the "family of man" can be united'.

2. 'To raise money for the provision of recreational facilities in London'

3. 'To help London tourism'.

4. 'To have fun and provide some happiness and sense of achievement in a troubled world'.

In the first objective the ethos of the EPs is clearly a 'family' in itself, epitomised by the Ever-presents website, their media coverage as a recognisable group and their camaraderie throughout the year. Their own families support en route has been an 'Ever-present' over the years too.

London tourism has undoubtedly been given a boost albeit in a small way by the involvement of the EPs, their families, friends, clubs and supporters over 33 years.

In many of the EP contributions, the fourth objectives shines through clearly whereby *'having fun'* and enjoying a *'sense of achievement'* is an often mentioned motif by the EPs. One EP, 'The Galloping Gourmet' has over the years entertained spectators and runners alike by tossing pancakes, running 3 legged, carrying an egg on a spoon, running with a zimmer frame and dressed as a Bustard, in the course of raising charity funds. Other EPs have also enjoyed the *'fun'* link within the Marathon family.

The second objective referring to *'raising money'* is close to the mind and soul of the EPs when seen through the eyes of the media in its many forms. Media coverage not only publicised the amounts raised and the trials the EPs went through to raise it but also their reasons for doing it, either by helping the community or by sponsoring those organisations who have helped individuals and groups.

EPs have shown many examples of how they have used their running, sports and allied skills in service to their communities both by word and deed, at club, local or in a national context. **Chapter 9** describes, time after time the many ways that the EPs have given up their time and skills in community service. A prime example of this is *'Director General'* Jan Hildreth, with his charity roles and volunteering across the public domain.

The significance of being an Ever-present
What follows are quotes about being an EP.

Jeff Aston *"not taking part is not an option, I have to complete the distance to keep up the record"*

In 2005 despite leg blood clots, Mike Wilkinson was determined to run his 25th consecutive London

Rainer Burchett's take is *"we must all share some sort of dogged determination to keep going no matter what"*.

Chris Finill's tongue firmly in cheek - *"it would have been a lot easier if I'd have missed one of the early Londons, although the pressure (of being an EP) does give context and purpose to the training three decades down the line"*.

Mike Peace *"It's a unique band of runners in a club you can only leave. We can do our part in making a continuing connection to the unique quality of the (London) race"*

Jeff Aston is very proud he says *"of being in a Club no-one else can join"*

Dave Fereday says *"being an EP is the main target of my life and the all pervading reason for training and carrying on!"* Strong stuff!

Terry Macy feels *"to keep running all year and once a year to meet friends and family to share the enjoyment of the weekend of the marathon. I think people share my belief that I have been very fortunate to have had the health to be marathon fit for 33 years"*.

"I'm immensely proud of being in such illustrious company (as the other EPs)" says Dale Lyons.

'Doc' Mac Speaks says with a medical slant *"it's a bloody obsession, a compulsive disorder!"* He adds *"But I wouldn't run (London) if I were not an EP but it's a real status symbol and given the opportunity I do swank about it"*.

Bryan Read saw the London as *"a major part of my life that all my training was built around."*

Ray Johnson (a non-active EP) bemoaned *"it still hurts to see the EP list of finishers every year"*. His comment clearly shows how much being an EP meant.

Reg. Burbidge said *"It's a fraternity: no-one wants to see anyone drop out"*

Being an EP made Roger Mawer *"lots of friends all around the world."*

Being an EP, Dave Clark said *"was like wearing a special badge, it was never going to get any better or bigger."*

In the 2003 London Mick McGeoch was spectating when Chris Finill ran over and gave him a big hug. Mick recalls *"I just burst out crying, with tears running down my face!"* He wasn't an active EP anymore!

Ever-presents psychological profile.

An EP suggested that if you really wanted to understand the motivation and inner workings of an EP then you should conduct a psychological profile. Maybe they have a point but to do it properly would be too costly and secondly it would hardly be professional if it was done informally. It is a tempting question nevertheless because it does take someone with a complex mental make-up to embark, let alone complete some of things the EPs have done within their running lives.

Roger Low for example described his psychological profile as *"driven; able to concentrate and focus; willing to accept hardship, pain, heat, cold; (and is) a loner"* Couldn't this profile apply to most EPs? Well let's try to analyse the EPs mental make-up, on a strictly amateur basis of course.

Ever-present mindsets

First of all, we have heard that in order to do any marathons in the words of one of the EP's wives you must be *'bonkers'* while a famous gold medal Olympian told an EP *'you must be mad'* after learning he had run every London. Being labelled *'mad'* assumes you do things out of the ordinary or even extraordinary and of course most non-runners would agree that running 26.2 miles or even longer, non-stop is a bit unusual. The expression *'you don't have to be mad to do this (a marathon) but it helps'* is oft quoted by marathon runners.

Tom McCook ex President of Birchfield Harriers and a London Marathoner underlines the point. *"It is difficult to comprehend the extraordinary level of determination, single minded dedication, combined with a touch of madness to be able to be a member of that exclusive Ever-presents club for 33 consecutive London Marathons."*

He goes on to provide a telling quote from John J. Kelley, the winner of the Boston Marathon. *"We runners are all a bit nutty but we are good people who just want to enjoy our healthy primitive challenge. Others may not understand running but we do it and cherish it."*

So depending on who you ask about the mindset of marathon runners you will receive responses which can be viewed favourably or not. For example an EP may be labelled *'mad'* while others might say they are just *'eccentric'*. To run marathons you have to be *'selfish'* but why not *'single-minded'*? Are EPs *'aggressive'* or just *'fully focused'*? Describing an EP as *'focused'*, *'determined'*, *'bloodyminded'*, *'highly motivated'*, *'macho'* or even *'ruthless'* in pursuit of their goals almost assumes a dominant alpha profile. Another reason perhaps why there are no female EPs?

That is not to say all EPs fit this description, in that a single person with few binding ties can please themselves and have a free rein to indulge their favourite runs. Whoever they are, I suspect that they are few and far between, based on the lives of the present EPs.

Ever-presents and motivational theories

As (personal) motivation is the psychological element that gets runners through when all seems lost, a noted behavioural psychologist Frederick Herzberg espoused a theory of motivation in his book * **'The**

Motivation to Work'. This theory fits neatly into the EPs motivational pattern and demonstrates why they get through the 26.2 each year.

Although Herzberg's Motivation - Hygiene Theory was primarily work related for its justification and application it is also generally applicable to human behaviour and specifically to the EPs.

In essence, the theory states that people are really motivated by things they do for themselves and when they do, their rewards provide further incentives towards their motivational goals. In the EPs case, fastest times, improved PB's, breaking records, and feelings of accomplishment etc provide these psycho rewards.

These rewards are intrinsic, in that they are self imposed. For example, realising a sense of achievement; a feeling of personal growth, of gaining recognition; or a sense of heightened self esteem and self worth. Are not most of these satisfactions felt before, during and after a marathon?

No-one can run a marathon for us of course. And what satisfaction is there in taking a short cut? This happened in the 2011 Kielder Water Marathon when a runner caught a bus home from the 25 miles mark to claim 3rd place but only until he was rumbled by the bus conductor! What are the psycho satisfactions there? Certainly none for the cheat!

* **Herzberg's 'Motivation to Work'** is a treatise combining many of the motivational theories of the 20th Century. From the traditional Financial needs school of motivation espoused by Frederick Taylor, through to the Social Needs motivators such as Douglas McGregor, onto the Psychological Needs school lead by Abraham Maslow and finally into the 1960's and Herzberg's Enlightened Management school.

His motivational concepts for developing more enlightened management employment systems were successfully installed in a number of large organisations such as Volvo in Sweden and Hewlett Packard in the USA. In recent years a new greenfield factory in Bristol UK based its management systems on Herzberg's concepts.

The support team is the key

One cannot talk about the EPs success without giving credit to their backup team. Without this support they would have found it difficult to complete the marathons they did with the same degree of preparedness and enjoyment pre or post marathon.
Teams of family, friends, colleagues and club supporters provide the essential ingredients to the mix that encourages, motivates and facilitates the EPs before, during and after their runs.

Let's face it, any family containing an EP has to give them lots of support and TLC to ensure they can get to the start every year. Again, it is perhaps not surprising that there were no women EPs, with their competing loyalties between running and family commitments.

Who checks the EPs preparedness; who ensures they have the freedom to train; who is there to encourage them when they're flagging at the 22 mile mark; who provides the post race TLC and succour and organises the necessary R & R (rest and recuperation) and who gives them that glow of satisfaction and recognition for a job well done? And finally, who stands in the cold and rain for hours waiting for their heroes and loved ones to cheer? The Support Team of course!

A future role for the Ever-presents?

Once the status of the EPs had been recognised and formalised by Chris Brasher in 1995, the original 42 were subsequently given London Marathon recognition in the form of a 15th Anniversary Medal, a 21st Anniversary Plaque and in 2005 a Celebrity Dinner. In addition, the London Marathon underlined this importance with a full page spread in the 2013 Media Guide.

The EPs have an impressive fully functioning website under the watchful eye of Mike Peel which keeps the 39 remaining EPs up to date with current news, and records the results, times and photos after each Marathon. An example of EP camaraderie was a recent lunch in London that was organised by Steve Wehrle where eight EPs were able to enjoy a convivial reunion.

So, could anyone else benefit from links to this diminishing group as well as to the other non-active EPs?...What about charities using them as exemplars? They have shown to be resolute charity supporters over the years and like David Walker's example many EPs would give talks on their London experience in support of their charities past and present if asked.

Surely there are also commercial organisations with links to the London that could have a connection to their marketing and publicity campaigns. Let's face it the EPs have had extensive coverage over the years within the media world? (see **chapter 7)**

Is there also a useful role for the EPs as ambassadors within the London Marathon organisation itself? Time and again EPs have been the promoters of the London Marathon's mission, philosophy and organisation as seen in **chapters 3 & 4**.

But, would the EPs themselves want a more prominent role in these or any other promotions, or are they just happy in the knowledge that they were and are part of a rather exclusive club? Why not ask them?

A final thought.

The primary intention of this book was to provide a fitting tribute and record for the EPs and a celebration for their families, friends and club colleagues. In other words those who have been their most enthusiastic supporters over the years.

It is hoped that on reading *'The Real Marathon Men'* they will say *"The 'Real Marathon Men' is a fitting testimonial and record to a rather unique band of marathon runners!"*

AUTHORS NOTE

A limited audience or a wider appeal?

If I had not written the book it was a reasonable assumption that no-one else would, and after 33 years time was running out. Because I had been laid up for weeks with ankle surgery which hopefully would allow me to do at least one more London as an EP, I had been able to complete the book quicker than anticipated.

The original size of the book that I had envisaged has also been expanded mainly due to the amount of detail the EPs have provided, and made me consider perhaps the book could have a wider appeal than just to EPs, family, friends and clubs.
So who might those extra readers be and what has the book to offer? It providads an insight to the mindset required to run a marathon or even further, so could the appeal be to marathon wannabees?. It is also a guide to the greatest runs across the world.

Why not to sports-persons in the round such as physiotherapists, sports psychologists, trainers and medics. EPs are past masters on providing lessons on *'mind over matter'* sporting endeavours. Look at those who have successfully used the mantra *'no pain-no gain'* to get to the finish line.

Or why not to some of those 850,000 who have already run the London Marathon? Surely they might want to relive their marathon moments through the eyes of the EPs, some of whom they will have met in the London over the past 33 years.

ACKNOWLEDGEMENTS

Firstly to all my Ever-present heroes, contributors and helpers without whom the 'Real Marathon Men' would not have been written.

Grateful thanks must go to Adrian, Dick, Colin and Dagmar, my good friends and proof readers. Also to David for his Photoshop skills. Without their skills and patience the book would have been indecipherable.

And to Patrick for his ability to solve unfathomable problems.

To John Bryant who has been a source and inspiration by his advice and help.

To Geoff Wightman a London Marathon icon for his kind quotations and help.

To Nicola Okey for providing Marathon statistics and information.

To Mike Peel and Mick McGeoch for all their background data, statistics and assistance.

To Richard at Authors on Line for his unstinting advice, support and patience in bringing this book to print.

Finally and especially, to Janet my partner who kept my feet on the ground with erudite, timely promptings during the book's development as well as gourmet nourishment during my rehabilitation.

N.B. Please consider E & O E.

Appendix 1. Thumbnail memories 1981 – 1995

A RECORD & REMINISCE OF RUNNING IDIOCY 1981 - 1995
15 LONDON MARATHONS LATER

Question.1. How many runners have completed all 15 London Marathons? (answer below).
Question 2. How many runners have completed 17 London Marathons? Guess both questions correctly without cheating & Chris. Brasher will buy you a large bottled water.

MARATHON STATICTICS

1981 (1) 3hrs.10 mins. P.B. by 30 mins.! Freezing cold & rain. The first marathon dead heat. Dick Beardsley & ???. I run for a few miles with the 'Perrier' waiter who volunteers to flambe the pancake.
1982 (2) 3.09.35. A beautifully sunny day on the 9th of May. The first world record pancake run. Guinness book entry in 1983 edition. Nobbled at water station but saved pancake!
1983 (3) 3.12. Extremely damp and slowed by waterlogged pancake. Beat Arto Deeto (Nic Joseph) of Star Wars fame for #50.00 sponsorship to M.D.
1984 (4) 3.10.40 Failed in attempt to break 3 hours after cracking 3hrs in the Wolverhamption 7 weeks earlier (2.57.15). Very windy and hot. Brasher warns me to get off the front line.
1985 (5) 3.56. Wiped out again after a 3.01 in the Wolverhampton. Walked last 6 with sever cramp in a fast 90mins. Gnash! gnash! Shouldn't have raced the Dudley 15 the week before.
1986 (6) 3.06.48 New pancake record by 3 mins. & into the Guinness Book again. Ran with Pete Green (Birchfield) for 17 but very rough from 22 miles. Beat Ray the 'poisoned dwarf'.
1987 (7) 3.50 & 5.09 1st double London world record in 8.59 mins. To 'celebrate' my fiftieth birthday. Obviously losing my grey cells! After the normal marathon,was hydrofoiled down the Thames to Greenwich (not recommended for weak hearts) and Blackheath start. Finished with the team at 7.39 p.m.. & only 30 mins. behind the last marathon finisher.
1988 (8) 3.09.50 with pancake & beautiful weather. Harry Carpenter eats the pancake for #50 for M.D., then retires!
1989 (9) 3.50 & 4.48 2nd double London & new world record in 8.48 mins. In memory of murdered friend Pat Churcher. Accompanied by Centurion & Blackheath Harrier runners.
1990 (10) 3.44. New world Egg & Spoon record for Guinness Book. Beat the American holder by 11 mins. & ran 29.9 miles. Alan Oglesby ace egg protector accompanied me all the way.
1991 (11) 3.34.50 Wiped out! Another failed attempt to break 3 hrs. 70 mins. for last 6!*?#!
1992 (12) 4.17.15 Set World record 3 legged marathon with Dave Pettifer, tossing pancakes. Dave dragged me through last 6 in 75 mins.! Well knackered after skiing injury.
1993 (13) 4.54 P.B.A.B.L.(After broken leg). With crutch and pancake, in case of en-route hunger.
1994 (14) 3.47.20 Failed attempt to break the Egg & Spoon marathon record. The specially choosen guinea fowl egg lasts only 2 miles, demising on Charlton High Street. Good weather.
1995 (15) 3.58.33 New World 3 legged record. Dave Pettifer drags me round for a new 1996 Guinness Book entry.

Appendix 2. Research Survey Form

EVERPRESENT DETAILS.
Name   (Christian/ Surname)
Phone
Address
E Mail
DOB & age
Birthplace/ Hometown
Marital Status/ Family
Employment / Profession/ Business / Work (before retirement)
London Marathons Completed Main memory? First London memories? What does (did) it mean to be an EP?
Running Club
Marathons   Completed
Fastest Marathon (place & time)
Records (running/ triathlon/ Walking etc.) Incl. fastest times.

Guinness Records
Charities sponsored   **And approximate funds raised.**
Other international marathons
MOST ENJOYABLE MARATHON – (give some details)
Interesting story/situation from   **A MARATHON**   **experience.**   **WORST MARATHON EXPERIENCE**   **(give timeline and attach any**   **more detail)**
Other sporting interests / involvement.   **i.e. triathlons/ skiing RECORDS?**
Other recreational interests
Have you a photo and/or a media cutting you could provide?   **Have I missed anything out that would add interest to your sports CV?**   **If in doubt put it in as I will make the literary merit decisions. Any**   **queries please give me a ring or e mail 0121 455 8887.**   dale.lyonzs@virgin.net
Many thanks for your involvement. I'll most likely be in touch with   **follow ups on your information. No personal details will be used without**   **your permission. Regards Dale**

Appendix 3 1995 Letter 41 Everpresents .

Mr Micahel Peel
29 St davids Close
West Wickham
Kent
BR4 6QY

FLORA LONDON MARATHON 1996

10 August 1995

Dear Mr Peel,

London Marathon Ever Present

Further to your completion of your 15th consecutive London Marathon, it has been agreed that all 41 members of this select group will be supplied with a Guaranteed entry into all future London Marathons, for as long as their sequence continues.

Your Guaranteed entry form will be sent to you in December, and therefore there is no need for you to apply through the general ballot or via a Club or Championship entry. Those of you who still qualify for a Championship start (sub 2:45 to be achieved since 1 January 1994) should advise us accordingly. You will then automatically be allocated a Championship number.

We hope that your training is going well. We will contact you again in December and look forward to seeing you again in London next April.

Yours sincerely,

Alan G Storey
General Manager

Appendix 4 1995 Letter LM Medal

NutraSweet London Marathon '95
IN ASSOCIATION WITH BUPA

Mr Michael Peel
29 St. Davids Close
West Wickham
Kent
BR4 6QY

NutraSweet London Marathon
PO Box 1234
London SE1 8RZ

18th May 1995

Telephone: 0171-620 4117
Fax: 0171-620 4208

Dear Michael,

"EVER PRESENT" 1981 - 1995

Congratulations on completing your fifteenth London Marathon. You are one of a gradually decreasing group which currently numbers only 41.

We are pleased to enclose a commemorative medal together with a suitably overprinted tee-shirt. Please also find enclosed a jacket and sweatshirt from this year's event.

We will keep in touch with you and will monitor your future progress!

Hope training goes well for 1996 and beyond.

Yours sincerely,

ALAN G STOREY

The London Marathon Limited - A Company Registered in England No. 1528489
Registered Office: 2 The Square, Richmond, Surrey TW9 1DY

The London Marathon Limited is a wholly owned subsudiary of the London Marathon Charitable Trust Limited.
A Registered Charity No: 283813

Appendix 5. 2001 Letter LM plaque.

23rd May 2001

Jeffrey Aston
24 Clos Treoda
Whitchurch
Cardiff
CF14 6DL

FLORA

LONDON MARATHON

The London Marathon Limited
PO Box 1234
London SE1 8RZ
Telephone: 020 7620 4117
Facsimile: 020 7620 4208
Website: www.london-marathon.co.uk

Dear Jeffrey,

I would like to take this opportunity to congratulate you for completing your 21st London Marathon and I am please to enclose a plaque for you to keep as a mark of commendation for your success.

I hope you keep the plaque in the sort of place so that your family & friends will notice this and immediately ask about your wonderful achievement.

I am also enclosing a set of results for the Ever Presents who completed this year's Flora London Marathon. I am sure this will be of interest to you.

Next year's Flora London Marathon will take place on 14th April and I will be sending your Guaranteed Entry around early December 2001. Until then I wish you a well-deserved rest until the training for the 26.2 miles starts all over again!

Yours sincerely,

Donna Sterling

Donna Sterling
Entry Co-ordinator

Appendix 6. Letter 2004 Celebration Dinner

FLORA

LONDON MARATHON

Dale Lyons
8 Smithy Lane
Church Lawford
Warwick
CV23 9EQ

The London Marathon Limited
PO Box 1234
London SE1 0XT
Telephone: 020 7902 020
Facsimile: 020 7620 420
Website: www.london-marathon.

14th May 2004

Dear Dale,

Congratulations on completing the 2004 London Marathon.

After discussion with David Bedford Race Director, it has been agreed that we will arrange either a lunch or dinner for the 'Ever Presents' in recognition of the 25th year anniversary.

We envisage that this will take place in March 2005. Details will be sent to you with your Flora London Marathon 2005 guaranteed entry.

We are very happy to comply with your request for the 'Ever Presents' to start from the 'Green' start for this special occasion.

Yours sincerely

Janet Smith
Entry Co-ordinator.

Appendix 7. Letter BBC TV 'Heroes'.

British Broadcasting Corporation Room 5032, Television Centre Wood Lane London W12 7RJ
Telephone 020 8576 3942

BBC

Sport Development & Innovation
bbc.co.uk/sport

8 Smithy Lane
Church Lawford
Warwickshire
CV23 9EQ
19th April, 2005

Dear Dale,

Thank you for all your help in the making of the documentary, London Marathon Heroes, we hope you enjoyed it.

I hope you had a fantastic day at the marathon on Sunday and that you and 'the bustard' celebrated the 25th Anniversary in style!!

Please find enclosed a copy of the documentary with our compliments.

It was a pleasure meeting you and I hope to meet up with you again in the future.

Best Wishes,

Paula

Paula Davies

INVESTOR IN PEOPLE

Appendix 8. LM Report 2003 Brasher dies.

23rd LONDON MARATHON 13TH APRIL 2003

The great event was overshadowed by the death of Chris Brasher the London marathon founder. His wife was given the honour of starting the 40,000 record runners on a bright morning. It was rather too warm for running 26.2 miles from Blackheath to The Mall but not for the crowds gathered to watch the three starts - Green for Celebs, Red for Vets, Virgins Fun Runners and Foreigners and Blue for Elites and Everyone else. Paula (Radcliffe) our world record holder started at 9.05 with the elite women and decimated the field in a phenomenal 2.15 beating her own world record by an unbelievable 2 minutes; wheelchairs fizzed at 9.15 and the masses meandered out of Greenwich Park at 9.45.

My number was 30,008 in corrales 4 and way back down Greenwich Way but fortuitously I found myself 10 seconds from the start after the gun went along with another EVERPRESENT (those who've run every London). I'd done the training; viz. long distance races from 26 miles to a half marathon 3 weeks earlier so felt confident of beating my time of 3.53 in 2002. Ah how are the mighty fallen!

For the first 8 miles just passed the Cutty Sark and along the Creek Road in Plumstead I was cruising at 8.4 minute miles and on target for a 3.45 marathon. Then inexplicably my times lengthened - the legs were heavier and ankles ached and old gents and ladies and portly youngsters passed me. By half way at 13.1 miles my target had slipped to 9.5 minute miles and sinking rapidly. Was it the heat? Had I overtrained? Had I rested enough? Was my diet right? I couldn't figure and the more I tried to improve the worse it got. By the time I reached 15 and through the Isle of Dogs into Canary Wharf I felt ghastly with still 11 miles to go!

Survival time - drink plenty of water no improvement - try walking - even worse - have a rest - no I wouldn't start again!

Problem with going this slow after a 'decent' speed is the masses aren't very polite in passing - you collect lots of sharp elbows.

I was passed by Gorillas, Fairies, Spidermen, Wonderwomen, Father Christmases and a weirdo with False Buttocks - how embarrassing!

Fortunately I was past caring - by 21 miles I was bearly walking with 13.5 min. miling thinking only of the next step. Through the Tower Hotel over the Tower cobbles and into the City Road I could hardly raise an OGI ! OGI ! OGI ! but neither could anyone else. I was absolutely knackered and in bits.

But rescue was at hand - at 24 mile (15.30 miling that's less than 4 miles p.h.) Janet waved me down and supplied the 'Galloping Gourmet' chefs hat, pancake pan and pancake. So, after an alarming expletive which didn't phase the attendant Aussies I shot off down the Embankment tossing away, passed 25 miles around Big Ben to cheering crowds and up Birdcage Walk at something near 8 minute miling - how was this possible? At 24 miles I was fearing a 5 hour marathon time. But, under the finish line, being almost brained by an enormous 'bottle of sherry' and tossing still, I finished in 4.49.39 secs. with a bear bummed Adam (fig leaf in place) just 'behind'.

Off with the (computer) chip on with the medal and a quick interview with Heather Irvine who reluctantly ate a piece of pancake and I was loaded down with a goody bag containing 23 items, honest! I slowly changed standing up eating a Boost bar, drank 2 litres of water and made my way slowly to the 'repatriation' area on Horseguards parade and a well earned beer! My 28th London (5 more than anyone else). My 66th marathon in my 66th year. It wasn't as spectacular as Paula's record but finishing again for the 23rd London felt just as good – oh Yes!.

Dales Time of 4 hours 49 mins 39 secs. was 56 mins. slower that last year. He came in 17,410th out of 35,000 finishers.

WHO BENEFITS?
Dale raised almost £650 for 'BEAR ESSENTIAL AID' a charity that helps Ukrainian orphanages with Toys, Clothes, Medication, Medical supplies and Renovates water and toilet facilities with local labour in Ukraine. The present orphanage had 170 terminally sick mentally and physically handicapped children who live only 40 km. from Chernobyl the site of the worst nuclear power disaster in history.

Dale (Galloping Gourmet) Lyons

Appendix 9 London sponsors 1981 2013

History of the London Marathon

Sponsor history

The sponsorship history of the London Marathon closely reflects the history of nearly all athletics marketing over the last quarter of a century. The £75,000 supplied by Gillette for the first race, compared to the £17 million budget being injected by Virgin between 2010 and 2014, tells of the rise of professionalism in athletics and the importance of funding.

Get more details of the new sponsorship deal between Virgin and the London Marathon, or read on to find out about the other companies to sponsor the London Marathon.

1981 - 1983 Gillette

From the outset in 1981 it was clear that funding for the London Marathon would have to come from the private sector, and sports agencies were asked to find the race a sponsor. West Nally came up with Gillette who funded the race for the first three years. In 1981 they paid £75,000 to be the title sponsor, and delighted with the increased exposure, continued to sponsor the race for another 2 years.

The stakes were raised in 1982 when a cataclysmic decision was reached by the sport's governing body, the International Amateur Athletic Federation (IAAF), to allow payments to athletes. In one stroke the era of amateur athletics came to an end. From now on the elite would expect to be paid, and marathons the world over would vie for their services. Inflation was on the cards and robust sponsorship would be vital.

1984 - 1988 Mars

Following the 1983 London Marathon, a two year contract was signed with Mars for £150,000, index-linked, which rose to £217,000 by 1985. For 1986 that figure rose to £350,000. Professionalism had well and truly taken hold.

1989 - 1992 ADT

Six companies presented their proposals to the London Marathon board, hoping to become the new sponsor in 1989. ADT, led by Michael Ashcroft, was the winner. Although the total sponsorship figure was never disclosed, ADT's financial support played an instrumental role in the London Marathon being selected by the IAAF to host the prestigious World Marathon Cup in 1991.

1993 - 1995 NutraSweet

By the time ADT's sponsorship came to an end in 1992, the London Marathon was firmly established as one of the world's leading marathons. Interest in sponsoring the event was greater than ever and NutraSweet were selected as the new sponsor. The partnership between NutraSweet and the London Marathon was a strong and professional one, establishing new levels of excellence in both the organisation of the race, and the behind-the-scenes administration. As a result of this successful partnership, the race witnessed record entry figures and the extension of the course to a spectacular new finish - The Mall, with Buckingham Palace as the backdrop.

1996 - 2009 Flora

The choice of Flora for sponsor in 1996 proved to be a smart move, and the longest sponsorship period in the London Marathon's history began, lasting 14 years in total. The London Marathon matured a lot during this period, and the race saw the rise of lots of new initiatives - most importantly the increased focus on charity fundraising.

During Flora's sponsorship, runners raised hundreds of millions of pounds for good causes, and the event became the largest annual fundraising event in the World. 2006 also saw the London Marathon forming the World Marathon Majors group along with the Berlin, Boston, Chicago and New York Marathons.

2010 - 2014 Virgin

Virgin Money were so inspired by the London Marathon's commitment to raising money for charity that they wanted to get involved and lend their financial expertise in an ambition to help the runners raise £250million in five years.

Virgin Money's commitment to this pledge got off to a great start with the launch of their not-for-profit fundraising website Virgin Money Giving. Virgin Money Giving has improved the way donations and Gift Aid is collected online so that more money goes directly to where it's needed most.

Since the beginning of Virgin Money's sponsorship of the London Marathon in 2010 we have broken the fundraising record each year with a total of £102.4 million being raised over 2010 and 2011.

Fig. 1 Everpresents 1981 Statistics

Name	Name	Club	Age in 1981	Rank	Time 1981
Christopher	Adams	Orion Harriers	38	13	02:49:37
Alastair	Aitken	Highgate Harriers	41	16	02:53:01
Jeff	Aston	Les Croupiers	33	14	02:49:53
Geoffrey	Balfour	Huncote Harriers		9	02:45:00
Reginald	Brown	SLH	49	27	03:07:38
Reginald	Burbidge	Highgate Harriers	55	41	03:54:17
Rainer	Burchett	Shaftesbury Barnet Harriers	41	22	02:58:30
Dr Harold	Chadwick	Bournemouth /TH&H	34	1	02:24:10
David	Clark	Newbury AC	45	17	02:53:55
Charles	Cousens	Vale of Aylesbury	38	21	02:58:13
Patrick	Dobbs	Thurrock Harriers	42	8	02:41:37
Erik	Falck-Therkelsen	Woking AC	40	23	02:59:59
David	Fereday	Barnet & District	42	32	03:13:55
Chris	Finill	Harrow AC	22	4	02:32:55
Derek	Fisher	Newport Harriers	45	19	02:56:22
Jeffrey	Gordon	Thames H&H	47	31	03:13:42
Peter	Greenwood	Canterbury Harriers AC	38	10	02:46:53
John	Hanscombe	Ranelagh Harriers	45	18	02:54:29
Jan	Hildreth	Thames H&H	48	36	03:25:37
Raymond	Johnson	Kimberley & Dist. Striders	48	29	03:11:00
Kenneth	Jones	Orion Harriers	47	34	03:18:37
Max	Jones	Birchfield Harriers	53	40	03:51:52
John	Legge	Orion Harriers	50	24	03:02:35
Roger	Low	Highgate Harriers	37	11	02:47:55
Dale	Lyons	Massey Ferguson RC	44	28	03:10:03
Terence	Macey	New Eltham Joggers	32	33	03:17:56
Lionel	Mann	Belgrave Harriers	40	25	03:06:07
Don	Martin	Royal Parks Police	40	42	04:10:00
Roger	Mawer	Lowestoft	40	20	02:58:04
Mick	McGeoch	Les Croupiers	25	2	02:24:19
William	O'Connor	QPH	35	5	02:35:52
Michael	Peace	Ranelagh Harriers	31	30	03:11:45
Mike	Peel	Blackheath & Bromley Harriers AC	39	7	02:40:30
Derrick	Pickering	East Hull Harriers	44	6	02:38:38
Bryan	Read	Orion Harriers	40	35	03:24:05
Peter	Shepheard	Blackheath Harriers	38	3	02:29:47
Dr Malcolm	Speake	Biddleston Bounders	39	12	02:47:58
Michael	Starr	St.Albans Striders	37	38	03:47:11
Tony	Tillbrooke	Victory AC	41	37	03:42:24
David	Walker	Chalfont & Chiltern	35	26	03:06:11
Steve	Wehrle	Dulwich Runners AC	32	39	03:51:26
Michael	Wilkinson	Duke Street Runners	42	15	02:52:51

INDEX

33 Sycamore 10, 168
Adams, Chris 67, 76
Adidas * Jog Log 148
ADT 179
Aitken, Alastair 28, 46, 71, 151, 163, 165, 168, 170, 174, 183, 209
All Blacks 144
Aston, Jeff 25, 38, 137, 154, 162, 165, 169, 174, 177, 201
Athens Marathon 131, 132
Athletics Weekly 67, 161, 168, 169
Balding, Clare 163
Balfour, Geoff 72
Bannister, Dr Roger 59, 78, 152, 199
Beardsley, Dick 28
Bedford, Dave 15, 88, 150
Belgrave Harriers 79
Belvoir Challenge 157
Benoit, Joan 193
Bhutan Marathon 143
Biddleston Bounders AC 61
Birchfield Harriers 67, 77, 164
Blackheath & Bromley Harriers 26, 36, 101, 203
Bourbon, Roger 27
Bournemouth AC 68
Brandenburg Gate 137
Branson, Richard 16, 180

Brasher, Chris............................12, 15, 19,
   35, 52, 127, 159, 212, 220
Brown, Reg.................................72
Bryan Read................................69, 174,
   175, 178, 189
Bryant, John..............................7, 18, 59,
   60, 84, 106, 168
Burbidge, Reg............................8, 77, 90,
   153, 161, 175, 177
Burchett, Rainer.........................12, 27, 98,
   99, 128, 129, 130, 135, 136, 137, 141, 143, 145, 149,
   174, 176, 184, 185
Bustard......................................57, 175
Canary Wharf............................46
Cancer Research UK..................174, 176
Canterbury Harriers AC.............83
Carrot, Jasper............................163
Centurion Joggers......................56, 57
Chactonbury Marathon...............157
Charles Cousens........................191
Chataway, Chris........................59, 86
Chelmsford AC..........................154
Chiltern Harriers........................54
Christiansen, Ingrid...................82
Christmas Tree Bribery Case.....60
Clark, Dave................................26, 96, 106,
   153, 162, 166, 174, 175, 177
Clark, David...............................174, 198
Coast to Coast............................42
Coe, Seb....................................70, 82

235

Comrades Marathon..................................141, 150, 155
Course 1 Measurer, Athletics.....................62
Cousens, Charles..43, 128, 131, 133, 136, 158, 164, 170, 174
Coventry Triathlon Club............................138
Cumbria Way, The......................................76
Cutty Sark..71, 82, 88, 102
Daily Mail..170
Daley, Tom..148
De Lisle, Richard..223
Disley, John...212
DLR (Docklands Light Railway)................46
Dobbs, Pat..28, 63, 99
Drummondville...130
Duke Street Runners...................................91
Dulwich Runners AC..................................41
Dumbleton, Kira...82
Duncan, Peter..27, 55
East Hull Harriers.......................................98
Eastern Evening News................................162, 166
Egg & Spoon, Fastest..................................159
Everest Marathon.......................................143, 149
Farah, Mo..31, 82, 141
Fereday, Dave..23, 28, 49, 131, 134, 139, 145, 147, 149, 174, 175, 192
Finill, Chris..8, 20, 22, 30, 32, 35, 66, 83, 128, 130, 141, 144, 146, 149, 155, 156, 159, 161, 165, 175, 199, 200
Fisher, Derrick..84

Fitt, Richard...223
Flora..180
Flying Fox Marathon...................................83
Galloping Gourmet..................................7, 56, 158, 167
Gebrselassie, Haile....................................168
Gillette..16, 179
Golden Gate Bridge..............................156, 167
Gordon, Jeff...59, 107, 134, 135, 151, 154, 157, 167, 174, 176, 194, 195
Goupillot, Colin....................................135, 223
Grantham 100k...60
Great Ormond Street............................174, 178
Green, Peter..164
Greenwich Park..14
Greenwood, Peter....................................83, 133, 135, 151, 174, 195
Guinness Book.......................................28, 156, 158, 159, 163, 169
Gwent Cross Country League.....................40
Hanscombe, John...93
Harlow Marathon...70
Heart of England Marathon........................36
Henman, Tim..195
Highgate Harriers...................................26, 37, 71, 90
Hildreth, Jan...84, 106, 133, 136, 163, 175, 178, 186, 213
Hill, Ron..87, 140
Hirons, Adrian..223
Huncote Harriers..72

Isle of Dogs...27, 42, 46, 57
Isle of Man Parish Walk............................50
Johnson, Ray...89, 134, 137, 138, 162, 189
Jones, Hugh..35
Jones, Ken..25, 64, 167
Juantorena, Alberto....................................33
Jung Frau Marathon...................................138
Kimberley & District Striders....................89
Kleine Scheidegg.......................................138
Lebow, Fred...19, 128
Legge, John..67, 72, 73, 75
Les Croupiers...25, 26, 38, 80, 83, 205
Lidington, Clare...163
Lincoln to Gratham 100k...........................157
Lionel Mann...79
London to Brighton....................................38, 60, 61, 66, 96, 102, 153, 154, 155, 169
Long Distance Walkers Association...........76
Low, Roger...25, 37, 65, 128, 133, 145, 150, 153, 205, 216
Lyons, Dale..7, 28, 31, 56, 128, 129, 136, 138, 145, 146, 148, 149, 156, 158, 159, 162, 163, 164, 167, 169, 176, 196
MacErlean, Neasa......................................162
MacIlroy, Gordon......................................83
Macmillan Nurses......................................146, 156, 179

Macy, Terry..51, 128,
    136, 139, 142, 174, 177, 201
Marathon and Distance Runner...................168
Marathon du Medoc.....................................134
Mars..55, 179
Martin, Don..20, 84, 106
Marx, Groucho...40
Massey Ferguson AC...................................56
Masters & Maidens Marathon.....................75, 99
Mawer, Roger...94, 131,
    144, 154, 175, 176, 205
Max Jones...67, 77, 150,
    151, 152, 156
McCook, Tom...164, 216
McGeoch, Mick..20, 21, 25,
    80, 88, 137, 140, 142, 145, 151, 153, 163, 165, 204
McWhirter, Norris..163
Moore, Bobby...70, 174, 176
Morton, Mike..155
Motivation - Hygiene Theory......................218
New Eltham Joggers....................................51
New York Marathon.....................................9, 57, 126,
    127, 165, 179
Newbury AC...96, 166
Newbury Weekly News................................166
Newport Harriers..84
Norfolk Marathon...92
Northern Ireland...25, 64, 167
Norwich City AC..91
NSPCC..174, 177
Nutrasweet..180

O'Connor, Bill..25, 45, 152, 167, 174, 175, 193
Okey, Nicola..17, 161
Olympic Torch Relay..................................64, 105, 167, 195, 204, 206
Orion Harriers...26, 64, 67, 69, 72, 76
Ovett, Steve...82
Peace, Mike...22, 35, 128, 129, 130, 133, 137, 150, 162, 175, 191
Peel, Mike..12, 21, 66, 72, 101, 129, 154, 156, 162, 164, 167, 168, 175, 203, 220
Peoples Marathon.......................................39, 169
Peters, Jim...70
Pettifer, Dave..28, 159
Pickering, Derrick.......................................98
Pietermaritzburg...141
Pirie, Gordon..86, 168
Ponte Vecchio...136
Pope, Steve...146, 155, 165
Radcliffe, Paula..31
RAF National Service...............................50, 58
Ranelagh Harriers......................................26, 35, 36, 93, 102, 150, 192
Road Runners Club...................................32
Rocky Mountain Marathon.......................130
Rotterdam Marathon.................................140, 183
Royal Parks Police....................................84
Salazar, Alberto...141

Shaftesbury 10 mile....................89, 150
Shepheard, Peter.........................86, 132, 150, 175, 185
Sherpani, Diane Penny.................143
Shooters Hill................................52, 201
Simondsen, Inge..........................28
Smith, Joyce................................86
Snowdon Marathon......................89
South Downs Way.......................61, 76, 150, 156, 164
South London Harriers.................36, 72
Southend Marathon......................94
Speake, 'Doc' Mac.......................22, 61, 151, 157
Speake, Doc Mac.........................187
Sphinx AC...................................56
St. Albans Marathon....................82
St. Albans Striders......................79
Starr, Mike..................................79
Stokes Bay Sailing Club..............95
Swiss Mountain Marathon...........138, 155
Taiwan..144, 156
Thames Hare & Hounds..............32, 36, 59, 68, 84, 163
The Ridgeway Path.....................76
Therkelsen, Erik Falck................25, 130, 175
Thompson, Peter.........................86
Thurrock Harriers........................63
Tillbrooke, Tony.........................100
Tippin, David..............................223
Tomlinson, Janet.........................223

Tomlinson, Patrick....................................223
Tower of London......................................27, 46
Tupper, Alf..86
Versarrano Narrows Bridge.......................9
Victory AC..100
Virgin Money...16, 180
Waitz, Grete...38, 86, 193
Walker, Dave..54, 178, 188
Walker, Hilary..33
Walker, John..19
Watford ½ Marathon.................................46
Watson, Lesley...70, 96
Wehrle, Steve...22, 26, 41,
  128, 129, 137, 140, 149, 162, 174, 197, 220
Wheeler, Ron..28
Wightman, Geoff......................................30, 210
Wilkinson, Mike.......................................91, 130,
  133, 140, 144, 151, 155, 162, 164, 165, 166, 178,
  202
Wilson, Harold...149
Windsor Poly Marathon............................69
Woking AC..74, 76
Wolverhampton Marathon........................57
Woodford 40 mile....................................60, 157
Worthing 20 mile.....................................60
Zabloudilova, Dagmar..............................223

Lightning Source UK Ltd.
Milton Keynes UK
UKOW05f1504270114

225340UK00001B/2/P

9 780755 216178